WHAT PEOPLE ARE SAYING ABOUT
THE ROOKIE AND JIM MORRIS'S
INCREDIBLE TRUE STORY

"The story of his comeback . . . filled me with glee."
—*Boston Sunday Globe*

"One of the most improbable baseball careers this side of Kevin Costner."

—*People*

"Astonishing. . . . Morris's accomplishments [are] just as amazing as those of the Hall of Famers."
—*Austin American-Statesman*

"Too unbelievable to be true."
—*ESPN*

"He relates his amazing story with humility and charm."
—*BookPage*

"Amazing."

—*USA Today*

"You can't make this stuff up. . . . A fabulous baseball story and a fabulous story, period."
—*Booklist*

"Inspiring . . . [an] incredible story about second chances."
—*Library Journal*

THE
ROOKIE

THE INCREDIBLE TRUE STORY OF A MAN
WHO NEVER GAVE UP ON HIS DREAM

Jim Morris
and
Joel Engel

WARNER BOOKS

An AOL Time Warner Company

Warner Books Edition

Previously published as *The Oldest Rookie*

This Warner Books edition is published by arrangement with Little, Brown and Company, New York, NY 10020

Warner Books, Inc., 1271 Avenue of the Americas, New York, NY 10020

Visit our Web site at www.twbookmark.com.

 An AOL Time Warner Company

Printed in the United States of America

First Warner Books Printing: March 2002

10 9 8 7 6 5 4 3 2 1

Library of Congress Cataloging-in-Publication Data

Morris, Jim.
    The oldest rookie : big-league dreams from a small-town guy /
Jim Morris and Joel Engel. — 1st ed.
       p.   cm.
    ISBN 0-316-59156-4
    1. Morris, Jim, 1964-   2. Baseball players — United States —
Biography.   I. Engel, Joel, 1952-   II. Title.

GV865.M648 A3 2001
796.357'092 — dc21
    [B]   00-064269

ISBN 0-446-67837-6 (pbk.)

Book design by Robert G. Lowe

To my wife, Lorri, who showed me the way
when I didn't even know I was lost;
and to the 1999 Reagan County High baseball team,
who knew me better than I knew myself.

—Jim Morris

To my daughter, Maggie, who has big dreams
and the heart to make them come true.

—Joel Engel

I OWE SPECIAL THANKS to several people: Sarah Burnes, my editor, who somehow turned me into a big-league author; Bill Phillips, who put me on the Little, Brown team; Ron Porterfield, who convinced me that I wasn't too old; Paul Harker, who kept me throwing; Roberto Hernandez, who helped me learn big-league baseball; and Steve Canter, my very own Jerry Maguire.

PREFACE

ONE of my favorite movie actors is Clint Eastwood. The characters he plays are men of few words.

Like me.

All my life I've been quiet. I don't start many conversations, and I answer most questions with a quick "Yes" or "No." You'd know that if you ever had the bad luck to sit next to me at a dinner party. Really, I drive my wife crazy. She's always trying to get me to talk more.

The truth is that I don't think I have much to say, and I don't like to say anything just for the sake of talking. Believe me, it took a long time to accept the fact that people I've never met are interested in my story. Whenever a reporter pointed a notebook or camera in my direction, I checked to make sure that it was really me he wanted.

After nearly a year, I've figured out that it's not me, exactly, who touches people; it's what I represent: the possibility that dreams from long ago may still come true, even if they look lost forever.

That kind of hope is important to the human spirit, more important than I'd realized before I started meeting strangers who wanted only to shake my hand and tell me, "Good going." I greeted the smiles of seventy-year-old men as they asked for my autograph, and I read the words of letter writers whom I'd inspired to chase an ancient dream. None of it had to do with baseball. These people were doctors and janitors, executives and retirees. What we shared were dreams from the heart as old as the heart itself. The only difference between us was that my wildest one had suddenly come true.

Why has this happened to me and not to someone else? I don't know. I do know, though, that this dream feels a thousand times more vivid now than it would have fifteen years ago, when I originally intended to live it. In those days, I was too immature to notice how few people are lucky enough to turn their childhood dreams into reality. I had to grow up first and learn to accommodate disappointment, like everyone else. Now, my whole life seems like a dream.

I've written my story as honestly as possible. Whenever I doubted my memory or it failed me, I drew on other people's memories to refresh my recollection. I also consulted documents and published articles and historical archives. The only things I've changed purposely are the names of a few ordinary people, when I thought that not naming them would be more polite.

In that regard, you may wonder why I chose to retell several moments from my childhood in which my parents may appear less than loving. My purpose in reporting these moments was not to shine an unkind spotlight on Mom and Dad; it was to explain the person I've become, because without knowing the full background, you may scratch your head over choices I've made. The truth is that I love my parents and forgive them for whatever they might have done wrong—just as they love and forgive me for nearly causing them a dozen heart attacks with my carelessness and daredevilry. They did their best, with each other and with me. I know what happens to you when your dreams break, but even with broken dreams they kept trying to do the right thing, fighting enemies they couldn't see and didn't understand. Some decisions they made were right and some weren't, but everything they did made me what I am. And for that I'm grateful to them.

THE
OLDEST
ROOKIE

CHAPTER ONE

THE FIRST THING you need to understand about West Texas is that even local video stores have announcement boards out front with messages like "Keep the Christ in Christmas."

The second thing to understand is that, if Jesus Christ himself were to show up on a Friday night in the fall, he'd have to wangle a seat in the high school stadium and wait until the football game ended before declaring his arrival.

In West Texas, high school football and religion are often the strongest links between small towns lying hundreds of miles apart. As you drive down two-lane highways that cut through scrub-brush landscapes littered with deer carcasses and the cars that hit them, your car radio is likely to pull in only two stations, country and religious—and both are likely to broadcast high school football games.

That's how it's been since before my father, Jim Morris, grew up in Brownwood during the era of black-and-white television. A city of about 19,000, Brownwood is in an area of West Central Texas where much of the country's pecan crop comes from. If you're there at the right time of year, when all the pecan trees are blooming, it's something to see. But pecans didn't put Brownwood on the map. Football did.

Even for Texas, the town's devotion to its Brownwood High School Lions is extraordinary. I can't imagine the people of South Bend, for instance, showering Notre Dame heroes with more affection than Brownwood residents and merchants do their home team. They treat football players like celebrities. You're lucky to be a great athlete in Brownwood, and even luckier to be a great athlete from another town whose father is suddenly offered a better job in Brownwood. Everyone wants to play for the Lions.

Yet my dad—who was big, strong, fast, smart, and had an arm like a rocket launcher—chose not to play, turning his back on a chance to be Brownwood's maximum BMOC, the starting quarterback. Glory, at least, if not a college scholarship, could have been his. But the new coach hired by the school board before Dad's junior year, 1960, came with a reputation for discipline. And Dad was allergic to discipline. Maybe he was trying to be nothing like his father, who epitomized self-discipline. Or maybe Dad modeled himself after James Dean and that whole Hollywood motorcycle-jacket culture. Whatever the reason, Dad preferred to drink, smoke, and chase girls—he was the rebel in search of a party. There'd be time for none of that if he had to practice football five days a week, four hours a day. Many people tried, but no one could sway him—not his father, not the coach. It didn't even matter that pretty cheerleaders favored football players, because his good looks, smooth talking, and come-on smile made him popular enough with other girls.

As it turned out, the new coach brought home Brownwood's first state championship trophy that first season. Grateful, the citizens of Brownwood tagged him with a nickname—"God"—though they whispered it.

Dad had missed playing on a championship team but felt no regret. To him, the world was filled with too many people who thought they were God. He couldn't wait to get out of Brownwood, where his mother was secretary at Central Methodist Church and his father spent his waking hours either volunteering at the church or running his menswear store the way Brownwood's coach ran his football team. College?

Not for Dad, not if he couldn't major in Pabst Blue Ribbon. No, what Dad wanted after high school was adventure. To see the world, and be paid for it.

He joined the navy.

When she was younger, Olline Ketchum liked to brag about her deep Texas roots. Way back on her mother's side was Sam Bostick, who helped capture Santa Anna after the battle of San Jacinto. On the other side was Black Jack Ketchum, the notorious train robber who shouted to witnesses at his hanging, "I'll be in hell, boys, before you start breakfast." Ollie, as everyone called her, used to wink and say that she had a little of both men in her. As her son, I know she does.

At eighteen, she was lissome and blond and stood five feet ten, with striking blue eyes and flawless alabaster skin. I've seen snapshots from back then and have to believe that, if she'd lived in New York, some photographer would have spotted her sitting on a soda fountain stool and put her on magazine covers. But she'd grown up in San Saba, Texas, population two thousand something, and had graduated high school without a clue about what path to follow. So she took her mother's advice and went to Brownwood for the summer to study cosmetology, renting a room with a shared kitchen and bath from the landlady next door. To her, Brownwood was the big city and offered big-city fun. And she was on her own.

It was the summer of 1962, the summer of Telstar and Diet-Rite Cola and the Houston Astros. One hot night when she should have been studying, Ollie freshened her makeup and put on something pretty. Running out to her car, she considered which hangout to visit first, Lion's Drive-In or the Dairy Maid on Coggin Avenue. A few minutes later she pulled into the Dairy Maid parking lot.

She spotted him, standing next to his car while talking to someone, the same moment he saw her. Wearing a tight T-shirt, he was tall, with broad shoulders and powerful arms. His wavy black hair was cut in a flattop. As he walked her way, she felt her face flush.

"Hey," he said.

"Hey yourself," she said.

He smiled as he folded his arms above her car window, and Ollie knew it was going to be hard to mind her mother's one and only sex-education lesson: "Keep your dress down and your panties up."

He was in the navy, he said, and would be going back to San Diego in a couple of days. San Diego? She'd always wanted to see it. Yeah, it's a great town, he said, but he'd be shipping out on a submarine— would be gone most of a year, to who-knows-where. That sounded pretty good to her.

His name was Jim Morris, and soon they had a date for the following night.

Over the next six months, Jim and Ollie carried on

a torrid romance—in letters. He wrote to her in San Saba from ports far away, describing what he saw, complaining about his superiors, and telling her about his dreams. He had the same easy way with words on paper as he did in person. When he came back on Christmas leave, he drove the two hours south from Brownwood every day. And in April, his next time home, Ollie got pregnant.

She knew it in May, since she was never late. After seeing a doctor, she called Jim in San Diego.

"Oh, good," he said when she told him. "It's what I wanted."

"It is?" she asked, thinking that the last thing he would want was to be saddled with a family. It hadn't been high on her list.

They were married in early July, on a miserably hot day, at the minister's house, with only a few family members and friends as witnesses. Jim needed to be back in San Diego in five days to catch a sub for parts unknown.

Nineteen years old and seven months pregnant, Ollie rode a Continental Trailways bus to California in November. She set up a furnished apartment near the naval base and waited for Jim to come back and for the baby to be born.

I arrived in January, weighing in at ten pounds. My size may have made it tough on my mother, but it saved my life when the naval hospital took thirty-six hours to diagnose my pneumonia. Treatment required putting me in isolation for ten days and left me with weak lungs and asthma.

It was 1964, and the Beatles were one month shy of Ed Sullivan. By the time they had the top five songs that summer, we'd already left San Diego and moved up to Vallejo, in Northern California, so my father could attend nuclear sub school. When that didn't work out, we were sent elsewhere, and then elsewhere, and then elsewhere.

At seven months old I made my first cross-country journey, from California to Key West, Florida, in my parents' new gray Volkswagen Bug that they'd bought with the money earned for Dad's re-up. Shipping their belongings ahead, they'd placed me on a pallet of cotton blankets that covered the hard vinyl backseat, and expected me to lie contentedly for five days. Somewhere outside of Phoenix, I stood up for the first time. Neither of them heard me, not with the noise that came from squeezing seventy out of that little engine and the 110-degree wind whipping through the open windows. As I prepared to launch myself through the space between the bucket seats, Dad noticed me in the rearview mirror and shouted to Mom. First she grabbed me and held me on her lap, then she reached down to consult her worn copy of Dr. Spock. Apparently, I'd just skipped five months of normal development.

By late that night, we'd nearly made it to Balmorhea, Texas, as forsaken a part of America as exists. Dad exited the interstate, hoping to find some Cokes and candy bars. Nothing was open. The only light came from the single traffic signal on the town's main drag. Mom checked that I was still sleeping. When she turned forward, the car was suddenly bathed in blue light, thousands of watts' worth. They had to shield their eyes. Dad commented that they must have stumbled onto an airport runway, and he put the car in reverse, but the light continued to blanket them no matter which direction or how fast they drove. They felt terrified.

Then it was over. The next thing Mom and Dad remember—and they're both clear on this—is driving fifteen miles an hour on a pitch-black country road, thirty miles east of where they'd begun, and feeling as though they'd just awakened from a trance. Dad checked his watch. Two hours had passed. "What happened?" they asked at the same moment.

Being too young at the time, I have no idea whether this incident actually occurred. What makes it meaningful for me is not the possibility that my parents had a close encounter; it's that this was one of the few things they consistently agreed on. In their twenty-three years of marriage, they were so much more often at each other's throats than united that I enjoyed seeing them defend themselves and each other against accusations of being crazy or drinking or taking drugs every time they told family or friends what happened that night. These were about the only times I really considered them husband and wife, and I was sorry when they finally stopped telling people the story.

Our first apartment in Key West was the tiny upstairs unit of a converted house owned by an elderly lady who lived downstairs with her grown son. The clapboard building had no air conditioning, only a small oscillating fan that didn't do much. Mom, who wasn't used to the humidity that made the late summer heat so much more intense, fanned herself and missed Texas. A week after we moved in, Hurricane Hilda struck.

Before hitting Louisiana and killing dozens, Hilda terrorized the Keys. All the naval wives and children were taken to the base and safeguarded in barracks while the men put out to sea in a sub for the duration.

When the crisis was over, Mom announced that she hated Key West. Dad asked her what she expected him to do about it. "The navy owns me," he said.

My parents were twenty-year-old kids who'd been drawn together by sex and had to marry because of it. That's the way it was done in 1963. The moment they conceived me, they forfeited the right to take their time deciding whether to spend their lives together. With their mistake growing every day, they felt trapped as much by what they were learning about each other as by circumstances. It seemed a blessing when Dad's assignment sent him to sea for several months. As soon as he left, Mom and I drove to San Saba for a long visit with her mother.

Grandma Frances was excited to see her only child's only child, and had bought a closetful of toy tanks, cars, and guns—the usual stuff you gave toddler boys. What Mom had forgotten to tell her is that I only played with balls. I loved balls of all kinds, big, medium, and small. Give me a ball and I would roll it, throw it (left-handed), bounce it, kick it, and catch it for hours; give me a toy dinosaur and I'd toss it aside, crying for a ball.

Mom or Grandma would take me to the playground, where I could play with other toddlers in the sand or on the jungle gym and ladders. But I preferred to chase a ball through the grass. The idea that this ball might be attached to a particular game with rules, like the ones being played elsewhere in the park, didn't compute. Nothing could have been more fun than exploring the physics of soft, round objects. That's why the older kids playing ragtag football and soccer couldn't hold my interest. They didn't seem to be having any more fun doing that with each other than my ball and I were having by ourselves.

Then one day, when the weather was warmer, a group of twelve-year-olds began playing a new game. For some reason, I stopped and watched.

They stood apart from each other, wearing leather gloves. One kid threw the ball at another, who swung a stick of smooth wood and struck the ball, which then flew in the air and was either caught or run after; meanwhile, either one, two, or three kids ran in a giant square. No matter what happened, the ball remained the center of attention.

There are moments and then there are moments. Most of them pass unremembered. Some become snapshots that form a kind of narrative. A very few stick in your brain and change your destiny. This happened to be one of those moments. With no conscious effort on my part, my brain just seemed to chisel this particular moment into something permanent.

Then Mom gave me the vocabulary to name it: Those kids, she said, were playing baseball.

I said I wanted to play, too.

By that afternoon she'd bought me a Wiffle baseball and bat. Hour after hour I insisted that she lob the ball for me to hit, or stand with the bat and let me try to sneak a fastball past her. But moms have their limits. So I learned to play by myself, throwing a rubber ball against the steps, catching it, and throwing it again. The constant *thwack* on concrete must have seemed like a Chinese water torture to everybody else. I assume that's why she bought me the Larry Sherry Pitchback—a large, rectangular frame attached to elastic netting that allows you to play catch with yourself. Silently.

All the activity accelerated my eye-hand-foot coordination. At a year and a half, I could do what athletic five- and six-year-olds did. If I'd had the same relative level of manual dexterity, I might have spent my days assembling models or taking apart and reassembling transistor radios. But I had no interest in anything else, not games, not models, not toy soldiers, not books, not even other kids—unless they played ball with me. And they didn't. I was too young for the kids who were good enough—they wouldn't be caught dead playing with a little squirt—and too good for the kids my own age, who could barely throw forward, let alone straight.

Dad's sub brought him back to Key West, and he was assigned shore duty. We moved into another clapboard house, this time on the bottom floor. (Good thing, too, because one day when no one was looking I managed to open the screen and fall out the window. It was the first of many accidents, and about the only one that didn't send me to the hospital. A few weeks later I swallowed a bottle of aspirin and had to be rushed there. Mom had been bleaching her hair at the time and of course didn't have time to wash the bleach out until the doctors assured her I'd be okay.) Having been gone so long, Dad was surprised by my skill level. First he watched me play, then he joined me. It wasn't a game as much as a tutoring lesson. He showed me the right way or a better way to do everything. I happily soaked it up, not yet knowing that there would always be a better way.

On the Christmas right before my third birthday, Dad called me into the front yard, where he proudly stood beside a two-and-a-half-foot-tall, green and orange battery-powered truck. "Watch this," he said, pushing the button. The truck began to roll forward, its oversized tires and powerful little motor taking it easily over every molehill and mound in its path. "Isn't that great?"

Dad's face beamed with the expectation that mine would beam too. And what boy's wouldn't have? What boy wouldn't love this truck?

Only one.

I looked at it and ran off screaming, in search of a ball. Dumbfounded, Dad stayed outside and played with the truck for a while before putting it back in its box. Poor Dad.

A few months later, Grandma Frances came for her first visit and brought me a gift. Not a toy this time, it was a junior baseball uniform—cap, shirt, and pants, all of which said "Little Slugger" on them—along with a tiny glove, a soft baseball with red laces painted on, and a tiny bat.

I didn't understand the point of a uniform, since I'd never seen a real team wear one, but I put it on anyway and begged Mom to play with me. She took me outside and agreed to pitch. The first one came and I connected. The ball soared far over her head. She cheered as she ran to get it, and when she came back I insisted on pitching to her. Struck her out. Fastball.

From then on the ball, glove, and bat became parts of my anatomy. I took them everywhere, begging people to let me hit or pitch. When they got bored, and they always did, I'd toss the ball up fungo-style and whack it, then run to retrieve it and hit it back the other way. Sometimes I pitched myself small rocks or bottle caps—whatever was on the ground. When darkness or weather forced me inside, I stood in the living room and practiced throwing the ball up and catching it in my mitt, over and over, hundreds of times, trying to see how close I could come to the ceiling without hitting it. In bed, I'd lie on my back and continue in the dark.

Nobody asked me, when I was three, what I wanted to be when I grew up. If someone had, I would've said I wanted to play baseball. I didn't even know you could actually get paid to do it.

CHAPTER TWO

MOM ONCE ADDED UP the amount of time she and Dad actually spent in each other's company during their marriage. The total didn't come out to much more than six or seven years out of twenty-three.

Calculations like that come naturally to military dependents. As a boy I once figured out that I'd spent more time in my mother's womb than in some of the places we lived. Most navy brats could say the same. The ones I became friends with in a dozen different places never complained about their situation. We accepted the fact that moving often—sometimes on a day's notice—was a fact of life. I didn't know that civilian kids lived differently until I was in high school.

By then I'd noticed that the military is not the most sensible career for a man who hates discipline, and I'd begun to believe that some of our moves had less to do with the navy than with my father's temperament. On talent and intelligence alone, Dad should have risen quickly through the ranks and retired with a lot of bars on his shoulder. He even had the political smarts. What he didn't have was the gracious disposition to use them. He wouldn't say "Yes, sir" when he had something else in mind, and couldn't suffer fools in silence. As many times as he'd get promoted, he'd be busted back again. What saved him from a few stints in the brig for insubordination were his wits and gift of gab.

It took a toll on Dad, having to suck up. He knew it, too, but traveling around the world in a submarine was a better way to support his family than working in his father's clothing store. When he was home—on shore leave or pulling shore duty—I could see the unhappiness on his face. And in his actions. He expected me to say "Yes, sir" and "No, sir" and not much more, and if I broke a rule on his long unwritten list, the price was high. Maybe it's because I was his namesake— "Jimmy," everyone called me—and he considered me his second chance to do it right. One day at lunch he said I'd stuffed my mouth too full of Mom's tuna fish sandwiches, then squeezed my cheeks to prove his point. The tuna shot out all over him. That time, I was lucky; he sent me to my room for the day. Some months later he saw me fooling with a box of billiard balls and poked me in the belly with a pool cue. I struggled for an hour to breathe.

When Dad was home I played outside as long as possible, and indoors I tried to keep out of his way by hiding in my room. Otherwise I ran the risk of saying something wrong or of saying nothing at all or of looking at someone the wrong way. Almost any offense could bring a beating with the big wooden bristle brush he used to clean his uniforms.

I breathed a little easier when Dad wasn't there, but Mom could step in as hanging judge herself. I remember leaving a milk carton out on the counter one day and her pouring the contents over my head before smacking me with a curtain rod.

In my mind, I deserved only one of the beatings I got, for shooting a hole in the floor with a loaded pistol Dad kept around the house.

Moving every year or so taught me to adapt quickly to new situations. It also kept me from making friends the way most people do when they're young; friends you grow up and grow old with; friends you may not talk to for a year or two and then when you do it's as familiar as ever; friends who vow to die for you. It takes time to develop friends like that. And it also takes the belief that you'll have the time.

My best friend was sports. I leaned on sports as

much as real friends lean on each other. Being shy, my heart pounded as we drove into each new town. Then I'd see a playground. I knew all I had to do was get in a game, and within an hour my best friend would win me ten new buddies. That's how it works for boys. If you're good, everyone wants to know you. And if you're really good, everyone likes you.

I wasn't quite four when we left Key West for San Pedro, California, a hilly port town south of Los Angeles, and moved into navy housing on a hill near the army base. I made friends with some kids who lived down the block. They were a little older but accepted me because I could play better than they could. Everything we did became some sort of competition to see who could hit farther or run faster or jump higher. One day we stopped in a vacant lot and had a rock-throwing contest, aiming for the "No Trespassing" sign from about fifty feet. I won. Next we decided to hit the "T" in trespassing. I was the first with a bull's-eye. Then we aimed at the bird perched on a wire about sixty feet away and thirty feet up. No one thought any of us would come close. But on my first throw, a palm-size boulder wiped the bird off the wire with a thud that was more horrible for being nearly silent. As the bird dropped to the ground, I felt sick. One of the boys began crying. Then I did, too, and ran home, and got a whipping.

Mom was pregnant then, ready to burst, with my

brother Kael. From my five-year-old perspective, her pregnancy made no sense. I'd lie in bed and hear my parents shout at each other that they'd married only because of me. So why were they having another baby?

Everyone in Texas had warned Mom that the marriage would never work out. They'd advised her to stay in a home for unwed mothers until I was born, then give me up for adoption and move on with her life. But Mom was as pigheaded at twenty-four as she had been hopeful at nineteen. She and Dad were going to stay married and work through their problems. The right thing to do was not have a lonely, spoiled, only child.

As it would turn out, Mom and Dad ended up having two only children, one athletic, the other artistic. When Kael was born in May of 1969, I wanted him to hurry up and grow, so he could play with me. But then I saw that all he did was eat, sleep, poop, and cry. By the time he was old enough to play with me, he didn't want to and I didn't want him to. We were too different, and from where I stood Mom and Dad seemed to like him better. Our lives intersected only by accident or edict. When Mom left me in charge of Kael, I'd get in trouble if he did something wrong. I saw him as one more excuse for a whipping; to him, I was the jackbooted tyrant.

In a six-month period we moved from San Pedro to San Francisco, back to San Pedro, and back to San Francisco, where we were quartered at the Presidio,

San Francisco's army installation. Outside its borders, with antiwar protests erupting across the bay in Berkeley and San Francisco itself becoming Peace Central, the army and navy were seen as equal enemies. But within the Presidio, soldiers and sailors still hated each other. Dad said that a sailor at an army base was like a bastard at a family reunion. He thought the only reason he never got jumped was that he always wore his diver's jacket with the patches, letting them know he wasn't some gutless swabbie. If they believed he trained SEAL team members or had some other hard-ass duty, there was no need to tell them he was rec services director on the Treasure Island navy base in San Francisco Bay, in charge of the swimming pool and billiards hall.

After a year we were sent to Waukegan, a town about an hour north of Chicago, on Lake Michigan. We were there just long enough to hate snow before Dad was reassigned to Key West, where we moved onto the naval base. The air was hot and thick and heavy, and you never stopped sweating. I loved it.

Three years had passed since we'd left, and everything looked different. I was now seven years old, and more shy than ever. For the first couple of days I rode my bike around the base, exploring. My exploration stopped the moment I happened upon a baseball diamond where eleven- and twelve-year-olds were playing. Pedaling like a pinwheel in a hurricane, I rode home to get my mitt, then raced back and watched from behind the right field fence, hoping that they'd notice me way down there and ask me to play. But they had about as much interest in me as I did in Kael. I couldn't figure out how to get in the game.

My answer came with a foul ball that rolled near my feet. I picked it up and rifled it toward the catcher—230 feet away. It reached him on the fly with plenty to spare. You could hear the ball smack his mitt. Every player immediately turned to see who'd thrown the ball so far. They saw a little squirt whose mitt was bigger than he was. After a few seconds one of the guys on the batting team yelled out, "Hey, kid. Wanna play?"

Do birds fly?

I jumped on my bike and raced toward first base.

"How old are you?" one of the guys asked me.

"Seven."

"Seven?! Hey, Pete, you hear that? He's seven. Man, I've never seen anyone throw the ball all the way home from there. You're up after Gary there."

I was in the game.

And from then on I was never out of it. We played all the time, and I played more than everybody else. I was usually the first one out there in the morning and the least anxious to go home at dark. I couldn't hit as well as these guys who were four and five years older, at least not right away. But I could do everything else as well or better, and if I saw a pitcher trying to take it easy on me, I backed out of the batter's box and shouted at him, "What're you, afraid of me?" That set him right.

Everybody called the field we played on The Diamond. It was actually a huge side yard attached to the house belonging to a naval officer named Carl, who had permanent shore duty. When he'd moved into that house the field had been overgrown and unkempt, full of rocks. Just for love of the game, he'd manicured it into a real baseball diamond, like Kevin Costner did in *Field of Dreams*, except there were no lights. Carl built it and people came. Everybody on the island—military and civilian—felt welcome to use it anytime. Carl insisted. You could see his pleasure in watching us play. He even umpired our games after work and seemed just as disappointed as we were when the sun set.

"Someday I'm gonna put lights in," he said, "so we can keep on all night."

School started in the fall. On the first day I sat quietly in class, waiting for recess—waiting to make friends from among the sea of faces I didn't recognize; all of them too young to play on The Diamond. At the bell, everyone rushed outside. But there were no balls handed out, no ballgames to be played. Instead, kids ran around and challenged each other to races. That was okay, too. I knew I was faster than any of them. Except, as it turned out, Tania.

A tall, thin, black girl wearing a dress, Tania moved

like a cheetah. Or did it just seem that way because she was beating other girls?

I learned the hard truth when she beat me, too. But how? Nobody my age had ever beaten me in anything. And especially not a girl.

The other kids were amazed that I finished as close to her as I did. Some of the boys acted as though I'd won.

"Wow," they said, "you're fast."

I had friends.

At lunch and after school, when the playground director brought out the equipment, I showed them what else I could do. Everybody knew my name. I was the first-grader who played on The Diamond.

But I couldn't forget Tania. I challenged her every day, lost every day, and wouldn't stop trying. It had nothing to do with her being a girl. It had to do with a voice in my head screaming that I should never be second best—the same voice that shouted whenever my father watched me play, or coached me how to play better, which he did whenever he watched me play.

Six months passed, then a year. Key West began to seem like home. We lived in a small house with an enclosed backyard thirty yards from the ocean. With Dad on shore duty, we looked like families I watched on TV—the Bradys and the Bunkers, mixed together like mismatched socks. Mom worked for the phone company and Kael learned to walk in day care.

What made the house a home—even more than Dad sitting in his chair every night—was the aging, dysplastic, black-and-tan German shepherd he bought for us. You could see from looking in his eyes that Nick had a human soul. I never felt safer than when I tucked myself up next to him on the floor, and he was never happier than when he was with me. Mom trusted me to go in the ocean alone if Nick came swimming with me. If Kael left his toys in the yard, Nick brought them in at night. For a long time the big mystery was why he sometimes smelled like fish. Then a neighbor said he'd seen a dog that looked a lot like Nick at the water's edge. He'd watched the dog swim in the surf, chase birds, and dig in the sand before trotting back to our backyard fence and jumping over it. The next morning we pretended to leave but instead sneaked back in a circle to see Nick jumping over the fence and heading for the ocean. What a great dog. He knew his fur would dry in the heat and salty breeze by the time we came home every night.

Month after month I worried a little less about moving, even when other kids came and went with their fathers' orders. I began to relax. It seemed that maybe our number wouldn't be called this time.

So the news that we were moving again hit hard. Then Dad said we had to leave Nick behind because we were moving to Connecticut, where the cold murders dogs with hip dysplasia. He promised we'd get another dog, but I wasn't consoled. Watching Nick's new owner lead him away was like lopping off my throwing arm.

We'd spent nearly two years in Key West. In that time I'd befriended dozens of kids in class and played with three dozen more on The Diamond, but the person I remember most vividly is Tania. I never beat her in a race.

Our move to New London, Connecticut, coincided with a historic event: the cease-fire that began bringing America's combat troops home from Vietnam. No parades were thrown to celebrate the war's end, and no one at my father's level in the military entirely grasped what the end of the war would mean for people like him. But talk that the armed services could be shrunk and that professional soldiers and sailors might lose their jobs did steal whatever relief or elation that pros like Dad felt about the war's end. So did knowing that we hadn't won. You could be nine years old and not really understand any of these currents, and still smell the cynicism. My parents drank too much and laughed too loud in social situations for there not to be something wrong.

It was four degrees with two feet of snow on the ground the day we drove into New London and found our new quarters in a townhouse complex that stretched the length of a block on the edge of a heavily wooded area. All of us agreed that it was nicer than anything we'd lived in yet. Dad explained that the navy had recently built new officers' quarters elsewhere on the base and decided to move its enlisted men into the old ones. We felt like millionaires. Two of our neighbors were a young officer and his wife who hadn't yet relocated to the new quarters. "I hope you're quiet and don't get into loud fights," the wife said to Mom the first time they met. (She'd been around a lot of navy marriages.) Mom improvised something polite and worried about what was going to happen when she and Dad really launched into one, as they would sooner or later. Before they did, the other couple almost killed each other in a fight that ended with him locking her out. Mom and Dad really enjoyed that, and the wife avoided us after that until they finally moved.

I didn't have to look far to find open playing fields. They were all around us—down the block, across the street, around the corner—but on our first day the only kids I saw playing were two boys who looked like brothers. They were next door in their front yard, throwing a football and playing a slow-motion, one-on-one tackle game in the snow. I watched them from my porch, letting them see I had a football, then went across the street and slogged through the drifts, throwing it and kicking it to myself. The next day they were out again, this time with a couple of other boys our age, playing two on two. And the day after that

they were with four other boys. I sat on the curb, waiting to be asked to play and missing Nick. It was hard
not to think about all the times we'd run around together. One thing for sure, he'd have broken the ice between me and the other kids.

After almost a week I'd had enough. So when their
ball tumbled off their lawn near me, I ran and picked it
up and kept running. None of them could catch me.
They chased me and shouted threats—they were
going to rip my legs and head off. I scrambled through
my backdoor.

Mom asked, "What're you doing?"

"Some guys are chasing me," I said, crying.

"Is that their ball?"

"Yeah."

"You took it. You bring it back."

"But, Mom—" I pleaded for sanctuary.

"I don't want to hear it," she said.

"But they'll kill me."

"Jimmy, just get out there and stand up for yourself.
Now!"

Mom and Dad believed I was too passive—not
Texas enough—and in fact this was the only fight I've
ever been in, if you can call it a fight, since I didn't
throw any punches myself. I brought the ball to where
they were waiting for me outside and they beat on me a
little, not too much, and when the beating was done we
picked teams.

On the first play I caught a short pass, faked right, sprinted left, and went untouched into the driveway end zone for a touchdown. The next time we had the ball I threw a spiral from near our own end zone into the opponents'. Another touchdown.

After that we were all friends, members of the neighborhood posse—black, brown, white, and yellow.

We rode our bikes and played army in the woods behind the housing, sledded down the snow-covered hill on the street, played baseball and football, and stayed outside all day. The guy I liked most was Stanley, the best athlete. He was tall and thin, with dirty blond hair to his shoulders (he looked like me; we both looked like ugly girls), and came closer to being a real best friend than anyone I'd known. Stanley and I did everything together, but friendship didn't come naturally to me. When we weren't playing, I felt a little uneasy. What were we supposed to talk about? I made a better teammate than friend.

Most of the kids followed professional baseball, even in spring training. They listened to Boston and New York games on the radio, or watched them on TV, and devoured the sports pages. They recited stats and tracked trades and argued over who was more valuable to his team, Mets pitcher Tom Seaver or Red Sox outfielder Carl Yastrzemski. In stickball games played at dusk on the front lawn, they all pretended to be Pete

Rose or Hank Aaron or Vida Blue. Not me. I could've barely contributed ten words about Babe Ruth. The only thing I liked about baseball was playing it. I liked the mitt and bat; the size of the ball; seeing the catcher put on his gear; the feel of the bases under your feet; stretching and playing catch before the game; sitting in the dugout during innings; standing in the on-deck circle; stepping into the batter's box; swinging, sliding, catching, throwing. I loved baseball. It was a perfect game. Why did I have to learn anything about professional ballplayers to know I'd be one of them? "Jimmy Morris goes into his windup and . . . strikes him out!" I'd shout to Stanley, who was Bobby Bonds.

There was still a foot of snow on the ground in March, so we painted trash can covers bright colors and put them down for bases and had a great time sliding in the slush.

The snow melted in time for the start of military Little League. Everyone said that the best player was Chip Cunningham, an older pitcher for the Yankees who threw hard and could hit a ton.

I pitched and played first base for the White Sox. From competing against much older kids, I could catch anything thrown my way and hit almost any pitch. No one considered me a superstar, though, until Chip and I pitched against each other. I lost, one to nothing, but the run scored on two errors, and both Chip and I pitched no-hitters—mine with fifteen strikeouts.

At the end of the schedule the coaches picked all-stars to compete against nonmilitary Little League all-star teams from all over Connecticut. We did well, considering we were a ragtag bunch of navy brats from here and there, none of whom had known anyone else longer than a year or two. I won a game by stealing home in the bottom of the last inning when I slid toward the catcher who was waiting to tag me, then suddenly stopped my slide and jumped over him without being tagged. The crowd roared and blasted out of the bleachers. No one had ever seen anything like that. Neither had I.

Baseball season flowed into football season, and I started PeeWee football, which is to Connecticut what baseball is to Florida. If you were a player, you played football. It doesn't have the beauty of baseball, but it does have camaraderie and competition, and I couldn't last the fall without them. I remember being an acolyte in our church, wearing my football uniform beneath my robe while marching at a processional pace down the aisle to light candles. People snickered at my cleats as I passed, and the moment that last candle was lit I raced out the door and ran to the field, throwing off the robe like Superman, in time for opening kickoff.

Knowing your lifetime dream from an early age is like being caught in the tractor beam of a Klingon spaceship. The rest of your days you're stuck, focused on a single outcome. Moments and people and occasions that color ordinary life fade into the background. In their place is a hunger that gnaws at you all the time and can never be fed enough.

In some ways I wish that hadn't happened to me. I wish I remembered more about school than just the playground. I wish my memory were full of colors and sounds and shapes and faces. I wish I'd thought less about me and my dream. But until the dream came true, life wouldn't even begin. That's why events from my time in Connecticut are strung together in my memory like snapshots in a photo album. There's me, tackling a runner in a football game and feeling something give in my neck. When I come to, my coach, hovering over me, tells me to lie still and wait for the ambulance, which doesn't come until Mom, who's on the sidelines screaming, runs to a phone and calls the base commander, telling him he'd goddamned well better get an ambulance to that playing field in the next two minutes or she was going to burn down the whole goddamned base.

There's Stanley, coming over to say goodbye. His father's orders have come, and he and his family are leaving—that same night.

There's Mom and Dad pulling out of the driveway as Kael tries to take a toy away from Nick Two and gets scratched so deep on the cheek he could bleed to death if I don't run outside, put my fingers to my lips, and whistle to my parents who are halfway down the block. It's the whistle I've been trying to teach myself for a month.

There's me, trying to ignore the knot below my left knee that grows every day and the shooting pain down the leg that keeps getting worse.

It's this snapshot that starts the narrative again, with our move to Virginia Beach, Virginia. By the time we got there, I could barely walk. A doctor diagnosed Osgood-Schlatter disease, which boys get when they're too active and their bones are too immature. He encased my entire leg in a straight-leg cast and said it would be on for several months.

Several months of no activity.

I was eleven, and you might as well have shot me. On my first day in the cast I got a whipping for trying to skateboard.

For the first time I attended a public school and for the first time appreciated military discipline. At this new school kids ran wild in the hallways, blew up cherry bombs in their lockers, and picked fistfights for fun, even on the school bus. All that might have been tolerable if I could have played ball and made friends. Instead, I was alone and miserable.

Our house was near the ocean, at the end of a street that ran into the naval air station. It was new, but the builders had forgotten to put insulation in the walls. At night you could see your breath, and in the morning there was condensation on the furniture. I loved to stand outside and watch the navy jets fly overhead, always wondering why Dad never got involved with aviation. One time we argued in the kitchen. He told me to shut up. I swore at him beneath my breath and hobbled out one of the two doors. He went through the other one. By the time I stepped into the daylight he was waiting and jabbed me in the solar plexus. I got a whole new appreciation for Dad's acute sense of hearing.

My cast came off in time for baseball season, and I made the all-star team but got the measles before the game. I begged Mom to let me play anyway, promising I wouldn't go blind and deaf, which in those days is what people believed happened to measles patients when they didn't lie in a dark, silent room.

"It means a lot to you, I know," she said. "Get your stuff. Let's go."

Dad found out I played and yelled at Mom a little. She told me it was worth it.

When you occupy military housing, you're expected to leave the quarters in better shape than when you moved in. On the day before we left Virginia Beach for Hollywood, Florida, Mom yelled at me for riding my skateboard on the white tile floors that she'd just washed and was now going to have to do again, so I went off to play Frisbee with my neighbors. What I like best about Frisbee is chasing after a long throw that starts out way ahead of you. You sprint as fast as you can and keep running until you're moving faster than the Frisbee, and then before it settles to the ground you snatch it out of the air. I told my neighbor to really let one fly. He did, and I took off after it, going as fast as I could, head down in a race with a flying saucer. Then I saw the Frisbee sail over the short fence. There was no time to stop. I leaped high to hurdle the wire and in the same motion make the catch. It was the greatest catch anyone ever made. But the landing wasn't as successful. My toe snagged the fence top, and I crashed in a heap on top of my left arm.

The arm seemed to be hanging by a thin tendon. I ran into the house screaming, "Mom, I think I broke my arm."

She was standing on a ladder, changing a light bulb, and glanced down. "Looks like you did," she said. "I'll be finished in a second."

I'm not sure even my being shot would have rattled her, not after all my trips to the hospital.

The cast on my broken arm was a perfect bookend to the year that began with one on my leg. We left town the next day, and I haven't been back to Virginia Beach since.

Two years after Richard Nixon resigned as president, Watergate was still changing the rules of the game that the Vietnam cease-fire had started for guys like my dad. The public didn't want to fight anymore and the politicians didn't want to fight the public. Even with the Cold War on, nobody was getting elected on a pro-military platform and nothing looked better than to be seen as an outsider. One way to prove you weren't an insider was by declaring that the military should have a drastically limited role on the world stage. So what we ended up with, in 1976, was the paradox of America's military getting a lot of raspberries at the same time that America was celebrating its Bicentennial by throwing the biggest party in its history—a history that began with the military. Anyway, that's how a lot of military pros felt, including Dad. He'd been told that the postwar ocean had less room for submarines than the old ocean. What his country needed him for now that there was no more military draft was to recruit new sailors.

Dad had left Virginia Beach a month ahead of us to go to recruiters school in Orlando. Mom, Kael, and I met him there (after stopping to visit the Bicentennial train, a traveling museum of Revolutionary War history) in time to see his "graduation," then drove south together to Hollywood. We rented a little beach cottage that was small and old and had a frog living in the shower. Mom told Dad she was tired of living in someone else's quarters and since he wasn't going to be at sea anymore, she wanted a home of their own. We bought a house at 6600 Arthur Street and spent several days trying to get the bedroom that had been painted black a more lively color.

It was good to be back in Florida, baseball country. By the time school started in the fall the cast had come off my arm and I'd made some friends on the field.

Doctors had been warning me for years not to play on grass—not baseball, not football, not roughhousing on the front lawn, not even fooling around at a picnic in the park—because the allergens in grass were known to incite asthma attacks; they considered it a matter of life and death. Well, yes, it was a life and death. I would've died if I couldn't play. My parents knew that and never suggested that I stop. Since Connecticut I'd been taking asthma shots. You couldn't tell if they worked or not unless you knew how many attacks there would have been without them. How could you know?

One day after a game I came straight home and went to bed without even wanting to eat. That worried Mom. She made my favorite dinner, porterhouse steaks cooked in tin foil with carrots and potatoes, but I couldn't lift a fork. Soon I felt as if a cinder-block wall had fallen on my chest. I gasped for air. Mom and Dad rushed me to the military hospital in Homestead. The first epinephrine shot did nothing; the second did little. I kept wheezing, so they hooked me up to an IV and an oxygen mask. Mom cried when the doctors said I'd have to spend the night in the hospital like that. They wouldn't let her stay with me, and before Dad pulled her out of there kicking and screaming she warned the nurses that they'd better tape the IV tight because I tended to flail around in my sleep. I went to sleep finally and woke up a few hours later thinking that I'd wet the bed. I had—with blood. Blood was everywhere, and rising. I'd apparently yanked out the IV—which hadn't been taped down—and with the needle still in my arm the blood continued to flow like gas from a pump. I screamed for help and a nurse ran in. Mom showed up early that morning and put on a spectacular display of language that I think navy people do better than anyone else; not for nothing do they call it "swearing like a sailor." During the week I spent in the hospital no Rockefeller was ever treated better than I was, and when I came home neither Mom nor Dad raised the subject of my not playing anymore.

Good thing. If you're a Florida boy and don't play sports, you may as well be a leper. At Apollo Middle School, just down the block from our house, I played baseball, basketball, football, and ran track. I had friends and no free time.

The summer-league team I played on—in hot, steamy air that even nonasthmatics had trouble breathing—was named the Italian Stallions. (This was the year of *Rocky*.) Everyone else on the team was Italian, and all the people of Italian heritage in the area came out to support us. We had plenty of money from sponsors to buy the best equipment. Even when we played away games, local Italians rooted for the Stallions, not their own team.

In winter the Stallions became a softball team. We played in the state tournament in Cypress Gardens, won that, then went to the national tournament outside Atlanta and came in third, losing to a team from New York who must have lied about their ages because they all had mustaches.

Mom never missed a game, and Dad rarely came. He'd show up with the game in progress, and I didn't have to see him to know he was there. "Throw strikes!" he'd yell, and as I came off the field he'd tell me a better way to do something. In one game I struck out fourteen batters of the eighteen outs, allowed only one skimpy single, hit two home runs myself but struck out once—and all he talked about was my striking out.

When I entered MacArthur High, a group of Cuban kids decided they didn't like my looks and beat on me almost every day until the black kids, who appreciated the way I played football and basketball, took up for me. After that no one touched me, and my best friends were all black. Wrestling was as big as any other sport, and they tried to talk me into being on the wrestling team with them. Maybe if the object of the match was to wrestle for a ball, they might have convinced me, but there was nothing I liked about fighting one on one, even with rules and referees.

I became the second freshman in the school's history to make the varsity baseball team (the first was Carmine Cannoni Jr., son of the Stallions' head coach). Hundreds of students and people from the area came out to watch us practice, and thousands paid to see games. I loved Florida because Florida loved baseball, and I never wanted to leave until I was old enough to play professionally. With Dad a recruiter now and not out to sea, that seemed possible.

One day in the middle of the season, he announced we were moving to his hometown of Brownwood, Texas, where the high school didn't have a baseball team. He and Mom wanted me to play Texas high school football. That and the UFO were the only things they agreed on.

CHAPTER THREE

A LOT OF HOMES in West Texas appear to have dropped out of the sky onto the flat, barren landscape. That's what occurs to you the first time you drive through. You can't think of another explanation for why that weathered wood with the corrugated roof stands all alone in the middle of nothing. *Bleak* is a word that comes to mind. So do *why* and *how* and *desolate*. It's inhospitable country, hot and dry in the summer, windy and dry in the winter, and if you don't have the shade of a tree or the pleasure of a neighbor's company, you're left with the ghostly whooshing sound of trucks going somewhere else, past your front door at seventy miles an hour.

And yet when you reach Brownwood, you could

easily forget yourself and think that you've somehow entered a bucolic New England village. In certain areas of town, Cape Cod–style homes face green city parks whose winding trails are dotted with vine-trailing gazebos. Around the corner, in the shade of pecan trees, stands a Gothic stone building that looks like an English cathedral from 1500. Not until you round the next corner and see Mama Underwood's Fried Chicken and the Hickory Stick Barbecue to go and the Dr Pepper bottling plant does it begin to look more like the West Texas of your imagination. But you know you're really there when you discover that the greenest lawn in town is the high school football field and the most influential man is not the mayor and not the sheriff, it's the high school football coach.

Gordon Wood had come to Brownwood High in 1960, the year my dad decided not to play. The town was starved for a winning football team and the school board knew that their political futures depended on finding a coach who could deliver one. They found him in a much smaller community about eighty miles north, Stamford, where Coach Wood had just won thirty-five straight games and back-to-back state championships. High hopes aside, no one realistically expected him to win anything that first season at Brownwood; in fact, area sportswriters picked Brown-wood to finish fifth in a six-team district. But Coach Wood was as expert at motivation as he was at moving the X's and O's around the chalk board. His players believed in themselves and each other. They won that championship, and had won four more by the time I got to Brownwood in 1979. That gave Coach Wood power. Brownwood High didn't have a baseball team because he believed it detracted from the football program.

It is no exaggeration to say that my entire story is built on the consequences of that belief. If Brownwood had fielded a baseball team—well, there's no rational conclusion to the thought. Everything would have been different. Sometimes you choose your own destiny, and sometimes it chooses you.

Texas is a place where men have to prove their manhood. You can be a tough, like my father was, or a cowboy, or an athlete. But you have to be something. And on my first day of school I was nothing, and without sports couldn't prove otherwise.

In Brownwood, ninth grade was still middle school. That would have been fine—ninth grade is ninth grade is ninth grade—but I'd already completed much of the course work in Florida, so the principal decided that I would split my days between the junior high and high school. I began each day at the high school and ended it at the junior high, with no friends in either place.

By three o'clock that first day, I missed baseball

enough to cry. I thought of my teammates in Florida, how they were playing a game right at that moment. Lost in my daydream, I wasn't prepared for Darryl Hardy getting right up in my face and saying something and then pushing me. He was upset about this new kid no one knew who was taking high school classes. I pushed him back and someone came between us. That night Dad told me that he'd entered me in a baseball summer league. My first game would be on Saturday.

For the rest of the week I wandered through the school like a pariah. Kids stared at me and whispered wherever I walked because I didn't dress or act like a cowboy or redneck or nerd or druggie—none of the regular groups—and they couldn't tell if I was an athlete. So who was I? Most new boys who came to Brownwood were preceded by their reputations. They were sensational athletes from other towns who'd moved to Brownwood after their fathers suddenly received job offers they couldn't refuse. Me, they knew nothing about. It didn't matter that I had local roots as the grandson of Ernest Morris, because Dad hadn't left his mark on the field; there was no reason to think I would, either. Being six-three didn't mean anything; everybody's that tall in Texas. Besides, I was still skinny. Darryl and I circled each other a couple times a day.

What changed everything was my first summer-league game. (It's called summer league even though it's played in the spring because you only play baseball with the time that football doesn't take, and by midsummer football practice is already beginning.) As these things happen sometimes, my team played Darryl's team that Saturday—and Darryl was the pitcher. I hit the first pitch he threw over the lights in right field. Rounding the bases I didn't smile, pump my fist, or say a word. The next two times up I homered, and when I finally came in to pitch, no one on his team came close to hitting the ball. Darryl patted me on the back after the game, and by the time I got to school Monday morning most people knew my name.

At first my family and I lived with Grandpa Ernest and Grandma Alice, my dad's parents. Ernest owned a menswear store that was considered one of the finest in Texas. He'd begun there years before, working in the back room for someone else, and now it was called Ernest Morris Menswear. His clientele came hundreds of miles to shop there; thousands, if you count celebrities like Gene Autry. The store reflected his personality: disciplined and sober. Even then I wondered how he could have been my father's father. Ernest felt that working brought him close to God. The man could have pneumonia, but he was sure as hell going to get out of bed each day, put on his three-piece suit, and drive to the store. He worked from daylight to dark, then locked the doors, turned out the lights, and sat and drank and chatted with friends who dropped by; when he left, he went home or to Central Methodist Church. The more I watched him, the more I wanted to be like him. He was solid and genuine. He said what he believed, and even if you didn't agree, you respected the man's opinion. His words might hurt your feelings for a while, but you got over it because they came with no hurt intended; agree or disagree, you learned something valuable.

I remember the first time he rained his moral force on me. Mom hadn't picked me up from somewhere when I'd expected her to, and I'd had to walk the two miles home. That didn't sit well. When she came in I was furious and showed it. Ernest jumped all over me.

"Young man, that is your mother," he said. "And you will not talk like that to her in my house. You will have respect for her. I do not care what your father has done to her, or how he has treated her. You are her son and you will treat her properly. Is that understood?"

Yes, sir.

"Remember who you are," he said.

He said it that night and every time I saw him. I took him to mean that I'm a Morris and I'm not supposed to embarrass the family name.

Alice was just as incredible in her own way. She had graduated college years before with a 4.0 grade point average and worked her entire adult life as the Central Methodist Church secretary. Seeing her and Ernest treat each other with love and respect gave me my first appreciation of marriage and what it could be. She was a great cook, and just to spend more time with her I would sit at the kitchen table and watch. Her recipes were too complicated, but I still make Ernest's pea salad (peas, black olives, cheddar cheese, pimientos, a little mayo, and a few other things I can't tell you).

It was hard leaving there, but Mom and Dad bought a house near the junior high, at the corner of Sierra and Horseshoe Trail, one block from Wood Creek Baptist Church and a vacant field away from the Camp Bowie Sports Complex. With four bedrooms and a large den, our house was bigger than anything we'd lived in before. What I remember most about it, though, was not being home a lot; sports took up all my time. I'd made the track team, running the 100-, 200-, and 400-meter sprint relay (I was the only white guy competing in the speed events), and doing the long jump. Meanwhile, I continued playing baseball, hitting the ball farther and throwing it harder than anyone. You could say I was a sensation. But I got too little pleasure from my accomplishments. I felt more like the best-looking pig at the trough. Here in Brownwood, baseball season lasted only a dozen or so games, and no one cared about it anyway.

In the city championship game I played center field. The score was tied with two outs in the bottom of the last inning, and with a runner on first the batter hit a sharp one-hopper to me. I ran in, scooped up the ball in my glove, and launched a rocket toward third to nail the runner. It was one of the more amazing throws I've made in my life, and maybe the least accurate. The ball sailed high over third base, over the dugout, over the stands, over the adjacent field, and well into the parking lot—at least four hundred feet. There wasn't a person on the field—or the next field—who didn't stand and watch it go, like a shooting star in the night sky. We ended up losing the game, and when the coach chewed us out, one of the guys began snickering about the throw. It was contagious. Everybody but the coach laughed.

Dad insisted that I play football for Gordon Wood without explaining why he hadn't. He pointed out that he'd engineered a transfer to Brownwood, from where he would now recruit, just for this purpose. I don't know if he wanted to live out through me what he'd missed, but even Mom chimed in. In San Saba she'd been on the football pep squad, and she claimed that football flowed through her bloodstream. The thought of seeing me in a Brownwood Lions uniform, running out of the locker room onto Gordon Wood's field, quickened her Texas mother's heart. To play for Coach Wood was an honor, she said, and a great opportunity.

Opportunity for what? They'd brought me here to play football because I was good at it. But being good at something is not necessarily the same as loving it. I loved baseball, not football. Still, I decided to make everyone proud and went out for the junior varsity team, as a quarterback.

Coach Southal was cut from the same mold as Gordon Wood. He believed that something worth doing was worth doing a thousand times, and on the first day of practice he made me run the same play over and over. When I could not master the footwork, I slammed the ball down on the ground. Infuriated, he shouted at me with words that felt like knives. I wanted to throw them back at him, but Ernest's advice rang in my ears—"Remember who you are!" If Coach Southal hadn't sought me out in the locker room, I might have quit. But he hugged me. And smiled. So his message had enormous impact.

"We're not going to act like that on our football field, are we?" he asked.

No, sir.

I won the starting quarterback's job because I could throw the football from one goal almost to the other, but in games I threw very few passes. Instead, I ran nearly every play. After taking the snap from center, I'd watch for a hole in the line, then take off and slice between the guards. No one could tackle me. One game I ran for about 220 yards and five touchdowns, and the wins piled up. It seemed automatic that next year I'd be the starting varsity quarterback.

First there was basketball season. Booth was the varsity coach and I made the varsity team. In the first game I tripped and fell on my ankle. It swelled up right away and turned purple and bloody, but I played the rest of the game because he refused to take me out. The pain stopped me from sleeping that night. In the morning the doctor said it was broken. He put it in a cast and gave me crutches. I went to school and for two periods listened to kids make fun of me. At lunch I threw the crutches in the trash. When I came home I told Mom someone had stolen them. I learned that in Texas, you didn't get hurt. And if you did, you didn't let anyone see.

I don't remember when I first met Gordon Wood. Neither does he. On some level that explains why I became a first-string varsity defensive back but only the second-string quarterback. The first pass I threw after the first stringer went down with an injury was a ninety-five-yard touchdown pass. And still I remained his backup.

To this day I don't know whether I displeased Coach Wood or whether he saw in me some enormous potential he feared I wouldn't reach without his badgering. I do know he didn't approve of my baseball dreams.

"Your future is football," he told me. "If you try to make it in baseball, it'll be the biggest mistake of your life."

I said nothing because you didn't argue with Gordon Wood. His record gave him that credibility. It wasn't baseball or Jimmy Morris who'd built the stadium and put 10,000 fannies in the seats and another couple of thousand on their feet all those Friday nights; it was Gordon Wood. He had a vision of what high school football should be in small-town America: the best and surest way to boost student morale and citizens' pride. And he made no apologies for it. He didn't have to. He stood on the sidelines chewing blades of grass, orchestrating wins.

Where I made a real impact was as the kicker and punter. All those countless hours I'd spent alone as a kid, kicking a soccer ball or football up and down the field, playing a game with myself to see how few kicks it would take me to go from one end to the other, had paid off. I could punt the football fifty yards into the wind, and place-kick it sixty yards. One time during practice Coach Wood told the team that we wouldn't have to run laps after practice if I could make a field goal from God-knows-where; the spot must have been seventy yards out. I ran up on the ball and shellacked it. It had the line, but did it have the distance? Every guy shouted at it, urging it through the air. It tipped the crossbar and fell over. With whoops and howls, they piled on me. I was their hero. But my pleasure from that moment, and others like it, lasted only until I remembered who I was—Jim Morris Sr.'s son, who could do no right at home. Dad had a lot of opinions why I wasn't the starting quarterback. He must've been the best coach who never coached.

I hated to have friends over because Dad always put himself on his best behavior, acting witty and charming, making me the butt of jokes that they thought I thought were funny, too. It was less embarrassing to let them go on believing that than it was to have them come over again and again, by which time Dad would lower his guard and let alcohol and familiarity turn him into something obnoxious.

I took refuge at Patricia Bostick's house. Patricia had asked me to a Sadie Hawkins dance at church, and from then on she was my first girlfriend. But we were really more like best friends than hormone-crazed teenagers. We loved each other and held hands, like children, figuring that when the time was right—if ever—then we would pledge ourselves to each other; it would be worth the wait. She didn't press me to talk, to tell her what bothered me, and when I was with her whatever was bothering me bothered me less. Her parents treated me like their second son. I was welcome at their home anytime, and was there almost all the time. Patricia's dad let me pull up a chair next to him and just sit. Sometimes we'd pass two hours together in the evening without saying more than a few sentences about the weather. Brownwood's a small town. You can be sure he knew I just needed to feel embraced by a loving family.

Something about my relationship with Patricia seemed to tick Dad off. Maybe he thought it was softening me. Maybe he was jealous. One day I heard him ask Mom, "Where's Candyass?"

Candyass. I wasn't entirely sure what he meant by it, but there could be no doubt he didn't mean it as a compliment.

"At least I'm not fat," I said.

Dad had gotten heavy over the years. I could see in his face that he wanted to level me, but he'd stopped doing that when I got bigger than he was.

The next thing I remember is that he stopped recruiting in Brownwood and shipped out to the Middle East; something to do with the American hostages being held in Iran—or so he said. He was gone almost two years and never talked to me when he called home, the way he talked regularly to Kael. He didn't ask about me, either. Once, though, he insisted that Mom pass along a message: "Tell your other son that I've lost weight."

Your other son.

It had been a few years since Brownwood's last state championship, and the natives were restless. We had half-a-dozen boys on the team who were new to Brownwood. One of the new players was Tyler Taber, a quarterback. I wondered a bit about that, considering that several high school scouting reports were listing me as a blue-chip quarterback prospect who could run fast and throw far.

Before one of the preseason practices Coach Wood called Tyler and me together and said, "One of y'all is gonna be quarterback and one's gonna play wingback. Now what's it gonna be?"

It was obvious that he wanted us to compete against each other, like gladiators fighting to the death, for the glory that went with being starting quarterback at Brownwood High. But that dog wouldn't hunt with me. Coach Wood had the wrong guy.

I'd seen Tyler play before and thought he was excellent. But he couldn't catch or run, and I could catch anything I touched and run untouched in the open field. Those skills figured large in Coach Wood's offense, which used a wingback as both wide receiver and ball carrier.

"Tyler's good enough," I said. "Let him throw, and I'll catch."

My motivation was the team's welfare. And besides, this was football, not baseball. No matter how hard he tried, Coach Wood could not make me care more about football than baseball.

*   *   *

As a defensive back, I intercepted three passes and returned them all for touchdowns. As a kicker, I knocked home a fifty-yard field goal, among others. As a punter, I averaged about forty-five yards per punt and made all-state. And I was better than all of those as a wingback, averaging over thirty yards per catch, including a lot of touchdowns. Tyler was outstanding and we made it easily into the playoffs.

In the semifinal game I dove for a pass and was hit at the same moment by two defensive backs. My shoulder popped out of place, leaving my arm hanging uselessly. At halftime I went to the hospital, had X rays taken, and had my arm taped to my side. When I returned to practice on Monday, Coach Wood said, "Did the doctor clear you, you pussy?"

The state championship game was played in Austin against Fort Bend, a suburb of Houston. The only people left in Brownwood who didn't make the three-hour drive were a few policemen. On the stop sign at the edge of town, someone hung a hand-lettered sign: "Last one leaving, turn out the lights." In all, there were forty thousand people in the stands. Our players were almost all white, theirs all black. They were bigger and stronger, and favored by two touchdowns. But we were coached by Gordon Wood, and so were more disciplined.

I played the game using only my good arm and running only deep patterns. For one pass that Tyler threw a little high, I jumped and caught the tip of the ball in my palm—like Velcro—just as two defensive backs drilled me. Somehow I held on to it. Mike Kinsey, a lineman on our team and probably the toughest guy in all of West Texas, sprinted downfield and grabbed me by the chest pads. "That's the greatest catch I ever saw," he shouted as he lifted me in the air.

We kept intact Gordon Wood's record of never losing a championship game. This was the last of his nine championships, and when he retired a few years later with 405 wins, against 88 losses and 12 ties (an .800 winning average), the town rededicated the field in his honor. Today the Brownwood Lions play their games in Gordon Wood Stadium. Everyone calls it God Stadium.

Lou Gehrig's disease, amyotrophic lateral sclerosis, hits about one person in 100,000 every year. In 1980 that person was my grandfather Ernest. He first noticed some weakness in his hands and arms, then muscles began quivering and atrophying, but for a long time he refused to see a doctor; he said he didn't have time. So it wasn't until late the following year that doctors finally diagnosed ALS.

Dad came back from the Persian Gulf about the same time. Ernest's condition really affected him, as it did all of us. It's a terrible thing to watch a six-foot three-inch, 225-pound man waste away from the inside, but when the man who's wasting away accepts his fate with grace and dignity, you're duty-bound to do the same. We bought the house next door to Ernest and Alice so that we could help take care of him. Seeing my dad do everything he could for his father put him in a new light for me.

By 1982 Ernest couldn't walk. That didn't stop him from going to work and church. We would lift him up and down the front stairs, into and out of his wheelchair, in and out of wherever he wanted to go. For years he'd taken care of everyone else, anonymously giving Christmas presents to kids who would have had none, buying Thanksgiving dinners for families who would have gone without, and even making sure that Mom had enough of everything we needed. Now all we had to offer him were small kindnesses. And they weren't enough. Not for me.

"This isn't fair," I muttered one day as we all gathered around his bed.

Ernest looked up at me. You could see the mood change in his eyes. He asked everyone else to leave and when we were alone he said, "Who are you to know what's fair and what's not? That's left to God."

Ernest's illness colored my senior year of high school. I viewed everything that happened through the prism of his dying. Even being student body vice president was tainted by it.

Patricia had graduated and gone off to school at

Texas A&M, but I still sometimes sat in the evenings with her parents. With other kids making plans for the future, my academic counselor told me that I'd better make it as an athlete, because my average grades didn't qualify me for anything else.

I didn't know how to make my dream come true other than by playing as much as I could, and that seemed to be my ticket out when several colleges, including Rice and Texas Christian University, sent scouts to one of my summer-league games. I hit three home runs that day and threw 85-mile-an-hour fastballs. But I turned down their scholarship offers. In those days, student-athletes had to spend a minimum of three years in college before they could even think about turning pro, and I had no intention of waiting three years, especially if they had to be spent in school. Of course, I didn't have a plan B.

In the spring of 1982 President Reagan called the Soviet Union an "evil empire." Closer to home, I graduated high school, Dad retired from the navy, and the New York Yankees selected me in the eighteenth round of the June amateur draft.

CHAPTER FOUR

SOMEWHERE IN MY FILES is a letter from George Steinbrenner, welcoming me to the Yankees. Apparently a scout from the major league's scouting bureau had watched a summer-league game and filed a report read by all the teams. The Yankees, down to the lower rounds without an authentic prospect among those remaining, had nothing to lose and decided to take a flyer on an eighteen-year-old who could throw the ball in the high eighties and hit it a mile. I should have been ecstatic. Out of nowhere, without a bona fide plan to make it happen, the dream was coming true. Or was it?

By then I'd heard a little bit about how professional baseball works and learned that if the team drafting you doesn't offer a signing bonus, you don't mean much to them. They've gotten you for free, don't have an investment to protect, and treat you like house money; if they lose, no loss. What the Yankees were offering was the bare minimum: a few hundred dollars a month during the long season and the opportunity to work my way up a really tall ladder from the bottom rung. Still, none of that would've mattered and I would've run with the chance if it hadn't been for Ernest's health. Watching him get more frail every day put me in no mood to leave the state for the promise of a promise. Every time I picked him up I could tell he was losing more weight. He was down a hundred pounds by now.

I hadn't told the Yankees no yet when Jack Allen approached me after my last summer-league game. Jack was the baseball coach at Ranger Junior College, about two hours north of Brownwood. Like all Texas junior colleges, it's known as an athlete's school. The guys who played there, football and baseball, either hadn't been able to cut it academically at a division 1-A school or, like me, they didn't want to tie themselves up for three years. Jack himself was considered a top coach; he'd turned down offers to go pro.

As he walked up I saw he was carrying a radar gun. He was short and fat, about fifty, and had a cigar in one cheek and a wad of chew in the other. "I like the way you pitch," he said. "I'd like you to come play for me."

Jack talked about how good his team was going to be the following spring. He said he thought they could win the junior college world series, and that major-league scouts galore would be following the team wherever it played. He must have known something; his teams had won that championship in 1973, 1978, and 1979. Ellis Burks, for example, an outfielder who later began a long major-league career, was enrolled at Ranger. So was Kevin Brown, who would pitch for the Mets, and Jeff Franks, who caught for the Angels. (Pitcher Donnie Moore had been on Jack's 1973 championship team. He's best remembered for his role in the 1986 American League championship series between the Angels and Red Sox, coming in to pitch the ninth inning of game six. If he'd maintained the lead, the Angels would have played in their first World Series, but he threw a gopher pitch to Don Baylor, whose home run tied the score. The Red Sox then won the game and that series, and the right to play the Mets in the World Series. Donnie never recovered and a few years later committed suicide.)

"We'll pay for your school," Jack said. "Room, board, everything. You'll get a completely free ride."

"I don't know," I said. I wasn't being coy; I just really wasn't sure. The season didn't begin for nearly a year. Maybe something better would come along when my mind wasn't so clouded.

Then Jack explained that Ranger plays a fall season of exhibition games against the best competition around. I wouldn't have to wait until the following spring to play again.

He talked some more and walked off with Mom and Dad. I watched them from across the field. Dad kept nodding and came back to talk to me.

"Look," he said, "I know how you feel about your grandfather, but there's nothing you can do about what's happening to him. I promise, we'll take very good care of him. And you're only gonna be a couple hours away. You can come home whenever you want."

Ranger Junior College is about five miles outside the town of Ranger, population two thousand and something. It was established in the late nineteenth century to support a nearby Texas Ranger camp, but then in 1917 McCleskey Number One oil well blew into a 1,700-barrel-per-day gusher, and poor farmers became millionaires overnight. You'd never know that from the way Ranger looks today—like a boom town gone bust, with only a granite monument downtown marking the well site. Its junior college isn't much to see, either. The buildings are unimaginative rectangles set down in orderly patterns on grounds dominated by dying grass. Across the highway and adjacent to a snake-filled hillside is the baseball field that must have been slapped together with scrap building materials; its dugouts are corrugated metal, and its outfield fences are metal and some other stuff I couldn't iden-tify. Painted on it is a cowboy wearing a Stetson and holding two six-shooters. Behind the fence in right-center, next to the rodeo grounds, stands a dilapidated shed.

I enrolled anyway. My class load was thirteen units (including the one for playing fall baseball) of introductory English, math, history, and biology. Nothing challenging. I remember thinking that the classes had been designed as an excuse for athletes to pretend we were real college students. Whatever serious learning may have been going on happened beneath my radar. Of course, my radar was set on High Jimmy—me, me, me. If something didn't please me, it sucked. Like the cafeteria food. I hated everything in there but didn't have any money and so I ate peanut butter and jelly sandwiches every meal. The only good thing was my dorm room. It was in the football dorm, which had air conditioning.

I drove home to Brownwood at least two weekends a month, to visit Ernest. He was a sack of skin now but still a giant in spirit. He insisted on going to Central Methodist every Sunday morning, so we put him in the wheelchair and went. Everyone prayed a little harder than usual.

On the way back to Ranger on Sunday afternoons I always saw the same Texas state trooper in the same spot on the grass median of the highway just outside Ranger. He, his wife, and their toddler daughter would sit on a blanket spread out next to the car, eating from a picnic basket. Beside him was a radar gun, aimed at the traffic entering Ranger. When the gun flashed above fifty-five, he jumped into his car, ignited the flashing lights, sped off the median and onto the highway, ticketed his prey, and returned to the family picnic. Something about that bothered me—something to do with Ernest and life going on while he lay there dying. But I was going on with my life, too. Maybe that's what bothered me.

One night in November the president of Ranger came to my dorm room to say that Ernest had died. "Go home," he said. "Take as much time as you need."

I don't have any recollection of driving to Brownwood. My mind was occupied with being eighteen and knowing I would never again see the most important person in my life.

There wasn't a lot of wailing in the house. By then it was a relief not to watch him suffer and be brave for us.

Brownwood citizens filled every inch of Central Methodist Church and spilled out four deep onto the sidewalk and far down the block for his funeral service. Ernest had touched every one of their lives in some way.

As I listened to the minister and others eulogize him, I remembered when he used to take me during my vacations to the old drugstore for a soda, and we'd sit at the counter on those turnstile seats and stare at the wall of magazines and talk about being a decent person without ever using words like that; he had a way of making you see between the lines. It occurred to me that Ernest knew what my dream was, but I never knew his—or whether he even had one. Looking at him and the way he lived, you would've thought that getting up early, going to work, and taking care of people was life's winning lottery ticket.

"Remember who you are," he'd told me.

"I will, Ernest," I whispered.

Jack Allen wanted to keep his team intact. What he feared was the supplemental professional draft held in January, for guys who graduated high school or college in the winter. Even if you'd already been drafted and hadn't signed professionally—like me—you were eligible. That's why Jack pitched me only on days he knew major-league scouts wouldn't be watching. You could tell who they were by the radar guns.

Jack's mistake was to schedule a doubleheader, and his bad luck was that at least a dozen scouts showed up that day. It would have been foolish to overwork his known pitchers in these exhibitions, so he had no choice but to pitch me in the second game. Before handing me the ball he said, "I don't want you throwing it over eighty miles an hour." I said okay and went out there with the intention of pleasing him.

Throwing about seventy-seven miles an hour, I got the first two batters out, but the third hit my "fastball" to Louisiana. That infuriated me. Jack or no Jack, I couldn't accept playing half-assed. The fourth batter dug in and licked his lips, expecting a fat lollipop to float to the plate. I reared back and let fly. The batter looked stunned; I'm not sure he saw the pitch, which I estimated at ninety miles an hour. I was mad.

As soon as the catcher caught it, Jack called time and trudged out to the mound. With his usual wad of chew in the left cheek and an old stogie in the right he mumbled, "Well, you screwed me," then turned and walked back to the dugout.

I struck out that batter and the next five I faced. Jack was noticeably disgusted. He put me in right field. I actually preferred playing the outfield, because I loved to hit. My first inning out there, a batter hit a long fly in my direction. I went backward on the ball, back, back, almost to the metal fence, and reached up. The ball sailed over my head and struck the fence, then ricocheted off and cracked me on the head. At that exact instant, a bee that had been hiding in my glove stung me on the finger. I didn't know what hurt worse, my head, my finger, or my pride, and I didn't know what part of me to hold.

Jack called time and marched slowly to the outfield. He was spitting tobacco juice, smoking the stogie, and holding a complete set of catcher's gear. Jack and I were the only ones not laughing.

He dropped the gear at my feet and said, "I think you need this to play outfield."

My humiliation was complete. I figured my name was being crossed off the scouts' lists.

Maybe it should have been after that, but a scout

from the Milwaukee Brewers named Fred Beene con-
tacted me. He wanted to know if I planned to return
for the spring semester or did I want to play professional ball. I told him I'd rather go pro. He said his
team would like to draft me in the upcoming supplemental.

"As what?" I asked.

"A pitcher," he said.

I said that sounded good. He asked whether
$35,000 would be enough of a bonus to sign me. I re-
ferred him to Dad, then Dad and I talked and told Fred
that the money was fine. Whether the Brewers expected me to counter and would have paid more was ir-
relevant. I would have signed for half of that—less
even. It wasn't about money; it was about playing baseball and feeling that they valued me. My God, I was
going to be a professional baseball player! I'd waited
my whole life for this. Dad warned me not to lose myself in the fantasy, in case something happened before
the January draft. He was right. The disappointment
might've killed me. But with the draft scheduled for a
week before my nineteenth birthday, how could I not
see the universe as a giant lock whose tumblers were
clicking into place?

George didn't see things with the same enthusiasm.
He was a salesman in Ernest's store who'd been a
Kansas City Royals scout. When he heard about the
Brewers he began yelling about how I was too imma-

ture to turn pro, that I needed the seventy games a year college kids play in order to grow up and learn the game. "Hell, son, you didn't even play high school ball," he said. "Those boys'll eat you alive."

They sounded like the words of an old-timer who was out of step with the modern world. Immature? Me?

The draft date came and went, and when I heard nothing I began wishing that I'd taken Dad's advice not to get too worked up. Anyway, I had finals and needed to study; obviously I was going to be at Ranger next year and didn't want to flunk out.

The following day I walked out of my last exam of the semester. Jack Allen was waiting for me by the door. "You'll be back in the spring, won't you?" he asked.

"Sure," I said, then drove to Brownwood for the vacation.

When I got there the phone rang. It was Ray Poitevint, a Brewer vice president. He explained that they'd chosen me with the fourth pick in the supplemental draft and intended to bring me a contract and the $35,000 bonus we'd talked about.

Ray and Fred came to town a few days later. We sat at my parents' kitchen table with the contract between us. Both of them wore suits. I had on a checkered shirt and an old baseball cap. A few local reporters and photographers recorded the moment. Dad looked over the contract quickly and didn't stop talking, and Mom was speechless; she thought I was too young and wanted me to finish college before trying to play professionally.

I picked up the ballpoint pen and signed. The sky didn't crackle with lightning or flash thunder. The earth didn't shake. Afterward we all shook hands and Ray welcomed me to the Brewers, which had just come off their best season ever, taking the Cardinals to seven games in the World Series. He explained that I would be reporting to the team's spring training facility in Phoenix on March 9, and before that would be sent to the Los Angeles area for a two-week instructional camp.

"Only our top prospects will be there," he said, giving me plane tickets for both places. "We'll see you there."

I cashed the check that day and went looking to buy a car. "Whatever you do," Dad said, "don't buy a little red sports car."

He was working at a GM dealership and talked me into buying a Jimmy SUV. I didn't like it from the first day and took a huge hit selling it back a week later in order to buy a little red sports car—a snappy Toyota Celica with a monster stereo. I figured I'd be pitching in the major leagues within a few months and wanted a car that fit the part.

It seemed right to say goodbye and thanks to Jack Allen in person. I drove up to Ranger and found him in his office. There was a chew in one cheek and a cigar in the other. He took the news well, but of course he already knew. What I hadn't known was that he'd also lost Kevin Brown, Ellis Burks, and Jeff Franks to the draft. So much for his championship plans.

Mom and Dad drove me to the Brownwood airport in the midst of a sleet storm that almost grounded the plane. Mom cried. I didn't feel much of anything but eager. The prospect that I might miss home was as distant as my embrace of Dad. "I'll see you in Milwaukee," I said.

I was nineteen years old and had lived in a dozen places, none of them big cities. The blood that ran through my veins came from West Texas. It was Ernest Morris's voice I heard in my conscience, and I addressed the lowliest and most exalted alike as "ma'am" and "sir." A punk was someone who picked fights, and drugs were aspirin and antibiotics. If you wanted to push the fashion envelope, you didn't tuck in your shirt.

I was completely unprepared for Los Angeles.

The Brewers put up a dozen of us in a small motel in an area of the San Fernando Valley where hookers and wannabes paraded past liquor stores, clubs, and strip joints. This was when you couldn't turn on the radio without hearing "Valley Girls," and I remember thinking that the song was more documentary than satire. Young kids styled their hair into blue and orange and purple spikes that looked like one of those medieval weapons, and wrapped four-letter words around "omigods" in every sentence, no matter who heard them. It scared me, but not as much as the woman who wore a ten-foot snake and not much else around her. I hate snakes.

If it weren't for my roommate, Tom Candiotti, I might have left town and gone straight to Phoenix two weeks early. "Candy" was a little older and a lot more experienced. He'd graduated college and played in the minors, then blown his arm out. Candy was trying to come back to professional baseball after a year of rehab and had decided to ease the strain on his rebuilt elbow by becoming a knuckleball pitcher. He tried to teach it to me in the parking lot of the motel, where we played catch. It was about the only place we could play, because the El Niño rain came down in torrents nearly every day, and on the few days it didn't, the junior college field we were supposed to use was too muddy. Without money or transportation, we stayed in our room playing cards or at the local coffee shop. Half the time the power went out from the storms.

I've never met a nicer man than Tom Candiotti. He reacted like Janet Leigh in the shower scene from *Psycho* the first time I said something that made him realize I didn't know the minor-league system from astrogeology. But instead of laughing, he offered me a crash course in Baseball 101. I learned that the lowest level of play was rookie ball, and that if you played well there you were sent to either low-A ball or high-A ball, depending on whether you did really well. After that came double-A, then triple-A, then the big show—the major leagues.

"What's it take," I asked, "a year or so?"

"It can take years—five, six, eight, even ten years or more," he said without laughing. "And most guys never make it at all. Major-league rosters are only twenty-five players, and every year a lot of new guys try to take their place."

The more we talked the more I began to understand what I was up against. At every level you're on a team. The better the team does, the better for you. But you don't necessarily want your teammates to do too well, because they're your competition for the rungs on the ladder. Their success may be your failure, because not every one of you can make it to the next rung; only a fixed number of spots are open, and every new season brings a new batch of hopefuls. By the time you've made it to the top, you're standing on a couple of thousand dead bodies, all of whom had the same dream you did and no idea what to do with their lives if that dream didn't come true. Fewer than one percent of those drafted ever make the big leagues.

"I guess maybe I won't be in Milwaukee by the end of the year," I said.

It was also clear to Tom that I'd been blessed with a

great arm but had no real idea how to pitch like a professional. "You can throw the ball through a wall," he said, "but that's not enough."

He was right. Throwing a ball fast and pitching it effectively to young men who'd all been blessed with talent were as different as a wild stallion and a champion show horse.

"You need real coaching," he said. "You've never had any."

What Tom helped me understand was that I needed to approach baseball as more science than art. I'd ridden this far on talent and determination and luck—same as every guy around; all of us had been blessed with ability. Now it was time to go further and learn competence.

On one of the last days before breaking for Phoenix, several of us sat in our room playing poker as a storm dropped several inches of rain. The lights flickered on and off, then the power went out for the tenth time since our arrival. We all groaned at the darkness. I stood to open the curtains and let in whatever daylight had survived the black clouds. Pulling the cord, I jumped back in terror.

"Holy Christ," someone shouted. "That's Andre the Giant."

In the days before Hulk Hogan and Jesse Ventura and Stone Cold Steve Austin, Andre reigned as the world's most famous and popular wrestler. He was staring in at us, his head filling the pane from top to bottom, edge to edge. It looked like that *Saturday Night Live* sketch in which Dan Aykroyd played Jimmy Carter as a fifty-foot mutant, the result of a nuclear-power accident.

Andre must've wanted the company, but all of us were too stunned to do the polite thing and invite him in to play. He stepped back and crossed the parking lot, holding a six-pack of beer that appeared no bigger than a softball in his enormous hand. We watched him go into one of the rooms, then resumed our game. We didn't see him again.

Over the years, whenever I read about what a gentle spirit he was, I wondered why we didn't ask him in and felt sorry we hadn't.

Thomas Jefferson never played baseball. If he had, he would have written that some men are more equal than others.

To say that I struggled through spring training is to say that Jeffrey Dahmer had an eating disorder. I threw the ball the way I always had—as hard as possible—but unlike the kids I'd always played against, these guys teed off on it, like batting practice. And they were just the class-A players. Or lower.

I needed a curveball to make my heater more effective, so in practice I tried throwing one to catcher Mike Gobbo. Mike was built like a fire hydrant and had a great sense of humor; everyone liked him. My very first pitch landed in the dirt, bounced up sideways, and sliced off the top of his ear. Blood poured out. It took a plastic surgeon to repair the damage. I was devastated and sat out for two days to recover. Mike came back before I did.

Meanwhile, other pitchers showed that they understood the mechanics and strategy of pitching. Even if they'd just had high school coaching, they were way ahead of me; but most of them had already graduated college, playing for coaches who'd forgotten more about baseball than all my coaches ever knew. They'd also played seventy games a season to my dozen or so. And they were at least three years older. I was just nineteen, going on sixteen. Whenever something went wrong I shouted "Damn!" at the top of my lungs and stomped around the mound. It was hardly a display of grace under pressure. I couldn't even talk to Candy about it. He was with the double-A team.

Nothing about that spring training agreed with me. I'm not and never have been a morning eater, but early breakfasts of scrambled eggs, bacon, sausage, and toast were mandatory. So was signing in; if you didn't, they fined you. Was this the military or a baseball camp? I couldn't tell. And that was lesson number two: When you're paid to play a game, it's no longer a game; it's a business. The thought occurred to me four hundred times that I should've stayed at Ranger, where I was a star and knew my role. Here, competing against professionals, I had no idea what the future held, and the doubt clouded my thinking. There was no way out but up and through, because the minute I'd signed that contract and cashed the check, I forfeited forever the right to play baseball as a college amateur. My maturity would have to come as a pro. Either I lasted long enough to mature fully, or I washed out; there would be no middle ground. The pressure was enormous, and the more I tried to concentrate, the more wildly I threw. I'm sure guys looked at me and wondered why the Brewers had foolishly offered me any bonus money.

After six weeks of spring training everyone gathered around a bulletin board on which the assignments for the low-A, high-A, double-A, and triple-A teams were posted. My name appeared on none of them, as if I didn't exist. I was angry. No matter what Candy had taught me; no matter how long the odds were; no matter how badly I'd pitched; no matter how undeserving I was; no matter the fact that if I hadn't received a $35,000 bonus they would've cut me—I wanted them to send me to at least the low-A club in Beloit, Wisconsin.

Bruce Manno, the Brewers executive in charge of minor-league operations, explained that I was going to "extended spring training" in Sarasota, Florida, along with other guys who hadn't earned placement on a roster, to join with nonroster Baltimore Orioles on a team that would play other reject teams like us. One of the Orioles was Billy Ripken, Cal's brother. Billy impressed a lot of us by doing something none of us could do. He could smash a beer can flat on his head. It looked so great I tried it and gave myself a mild concussion. What a laugh that got, one that went on for days when the horizontal swelling across my forehead refused to go down.

I suppose you can't expect more from a bunch of males in their late teens and early twenties who were living together in an apartment complex across from the beach and had nothing to do most afternoons but swim, lie in the sun, drink beer, and chase girls. Not that I chased girls. I was too much in my own little world—Jimmy's World—for that. Jimmy's World was already standing room only. It hardly had space for a few beers with my teammates. Why did I feel so separate from them, if all of us shared the same dream? It wasn't as though I spent my spare time proving Fermat's Theorem or translating Homer from the Greek. I just didn't connect with them. Or anybody.

Or baseball.

For the first time in my life, baseball wasn't fun. Mostly it seemed like a chore. Maybe not being a hitter had something to do with that. Nothing in sports compares with feeling that magic *ping* in your hands when the sweet spot of a wooden bat connects with a ninety-mile-an-hour fastball, sending it out of the park at one hundred miles an hour. You watch it sail high over the fence, then you circle the bases, head down, not showing up the pitcher, just enjoying your 360-foot jog. As a pitcher in the American League, which plays with a designated hitter, I'd never experience that again. But every time I thought about quitting, something of the old witchcraft would reappear and I reconnected with that three-year-old boy who'd slept with his mitt; baseball again became child's play and a game. And I'd think: *This is going to work.*

You don't have to live in a dream world to chase a dream. But it's a measure of how asleep I was that I never asked how long we were staying in Florida or what was supposed to happen next. We stayed until the June amateur draft, when we joined with the new prospects in a rookie league.

Rookie ball was played in Kentucky and West Virginia towns like Bluefield and Paintsville and Pulaski that took six or eight hours to reach along mountain roads, in buses without air conditioning that reeked of thirty-five guys and one stuffed toilet. Choking, you'd roll down the window, but the hot, wet air stuck to your face like flypaper. Everyone had boom boxes cranked up loud—the black guys to R&B, Latins to salsa, white guys to rock and country. It was a cacophony. I lost myself in Stephen King novels that seemed less horrific than my reality.

Then you checked into fleabag motels and ate three

meals a day of burgers and fries, which is all you can afford on a six-dollar per diem and six hundred bucks a month. You played in small stadiums with so few fans that by the third game in a town you recognized everyone's face and voice. And you endured morons like those in West Virginia who threw watermelons at our dugout and yelled "nigger" at our black players. (It was our white guys who stood up and fought back.)

In my first game I gave up three home runs—in the first inning. And those pitches that didn't get swatted over the fence nearly knocked it down. Unless I walked the batter. No one could have pitched worse. Not even the batting practice pitcher.

I was crying when I got back to my trailer and called Mom.

"I wanna come home," I said between sobs. "I'm miserable. This isn't what I thought it was gonna be. I don't like it."

In her heart, she would've loved me to come home. But Mom always kept her commitments and insisted that others do, too. I remember playing on a Little League team that was so bad the coach stayed away from a game out of embarrassment. Mom went to his house, grabbed him by the collar, and told him in her best Texas navy slang that he was a worthless stiff and that if he wanted to wake up in the morning he'd better get his ass down to the field. He did.

"You stay right where you are," she told me.

"But—"

"But nothing. You made your choice, Jimmy. Now you stick it out and make the best of it." She hung up.

My next time on the mound I heard a little girl of about twelve shout to me, "My grandmother pitches better than you—and she's dead."

I wish I'd known that the Brewers' coaches weren't necessarily looking for me to strike out every batter and win every game. They just wanted to see growth and potential from a kid with no organized baseball experience. Knowing that would have improved my mental health, but I guess they figured I already knew what was expected of me, because I never asked.

I'm sure the scouting report on me discussed my bad attitude, but if it didn't, it should have. ("Morris, Jim: good arm, lousy head.") Pitchers are supposed to be even-tempered, not manic-depressives. They must never let the opposition see their vulnerabilities. If they make a mistake with a pitch and get tagged, they have to put it behind them and make the next pitch the first pitch of the rest of the game. If they don't, you can stick a fork in them—the way opposing teams did to me when I made mistakes. If I threw a wild pitch, allowing a run to score, I'd scream "Damn" and watch the next pitch fly out of the park for a home run.

Even pitching well didn't guarantee me a win. One night I went seven innings, with a dozen strikeouts and only three hits allowed—and lost one to nothing.

The next night Dan Plesac pitched, and not particularly well, but my teammates scored twelve runs in the first inning on the way to a blowout, giving Dan the win. I began fuming about this quarter-million-dollar bonus baby getting all the breaks and winning games he should've lost while I lost games I should've won, and on the bus back to the motel I threw a tantrum.

"Where the hell was that last night, when I was pitching?" I shouted.

Glenn Braggs, our huge right fielder whose hand was the size of my forearm, jumped down my throat. What kind of jerk was I, he said, to think there was a conspiracy against me?

I learned my lessons the hard way. I also learned them by accident.

One game I had tendinitis in my shoulder and couldn't throw harder than eighty yet was as effective as I'd ever been. That was a revelation and brought to mind what Candy had talked to me about—throwing as much with my brain as my arm. You couldn't rear back and blow away batters who had such acute reflexes and honed eye-hand coordination; you needed more. And this was only rookie ball. Hitters were going to get better the higher I went. I'd better, too.

The sixty-ninth game of our seventy-game season was critical. In the fight for the league championship, we were a game ahead of the second-place team, the Pulaski Braves, which had won about twenty in a row, including their sixty-ninth game earlier in the day. It was a safe bet they'd win tomorrow too, meaning that we couldn't afford to lose our penultimate game. If we did, the best we could do by winning the next day was a playoff against the Braves, in Pulaski—and no one wanted that.

My record at the time was two wins against six losses, with an earned run average of six-something. Our team was much better than that. I felt like the weak link. We had real stars in Plesac, who'd played at North Carolina State and would go on to be the Brewers' all-time save leader, and Braggs, who came from the University of Hawaii and led the rookie league in homers, RBIs, and batting average (he later had a pretty good major-league career). So it seemed odd that our manager, Tom Gamboa, handed me the ball to pitch that game.

A lot of players tried to talk him into passing over my turn in the pitching rotation. I was among them. That was like me, to believe that I didn't deserve his (or anyone's) confidence. Tom knew that. He knew my biggest problem wasn't my arm; it was my head. I didn't face batters with the belief that I would dominate them. I did it with the fear of screwing up. If Tom had passed over my turn in the pitching rotation, the message of no faith would have been clear and the effects devastating.

Of course, I didn't understand any of this, and for a

moment questioned his passion for winning, even though Tom showed it every game. Rookie league was the bottom of the rung for managers, too. The better we did, the higher he'd go. Just a few weeks before, we played the second-place Braves for the last time that season and were leading in the fifth inning with one out when the sky suddenly cracked and poured faucet-like rain. We sat in our dugouts, watching the field become a swamp, praying for it to stop so that we could at least get two more outs and make the game official. It stopped. The umpires said that we could try getting the field in shape to play. We did. Every one of us— players, coaches, and managers—looked like we'd been in a mud fight after two hours of working Diamond Dry, which resembles sawdust, into the muck. We called the umpires back out. They checked the field and canceled the game. Two outs shy of winning, it was as if we hadn't played at all.

Tom went off like a Roman candle. I'd never seen anything like it, and I'd seen him throw other fits. Not even my parents, at their most angry, ever put on a fireworks display to compare. Tom ran onto the field and screamed at the umps, spitting flakes and juice from a big dip of chew all over them. Translation: Didn't they understand how much he wanted out of this backwoods league?

It all came down to that sixty-ninth game. Tom

sent me to the mound, I pitched five innings and struck out ten, and we won.

Plesac pitched the final game. He'd never been on a championship team, not even in Little League. Before the game he confided to Tom that he'd dreamed all his life about being out on the mound and pitching for the championship, and he guaranteed he wouldn't let the opportunity pass without a victory. He didn't.

I wish I could say that this was a defining moment. It wasn't. Whatever jubilation we felt spread a mile wide but sank only an inch deep, at least among the players. Because more than teammates, we were competitors. Next year there'd be another dozen of us trying to sit in fewer chairs, and I couldn't forget that. I liked Dan Plesac a lot, but how happy was I supposed to be for him when he did well? That was the riddle. Answering it would be impossible until we were both in the major leagues.

The Brewers sent a few of us to Arizona to compete in the six-week instructional league for top prospects only. That someone considered me a top prospect came as a surprise. Unfortunately, my last win for Paintsville didn't carry over. After running every day in 117 degrees for an hour while wearing a rubber shirt to sweat off some weight, I pitched poorly from start to finish and felt miserable. My shoulder began hurting, and I asked Bob Humphries, our minor-league coordinator, to let me try playing first base; maybe I'd give up pitching. I said there were years in Little League and summer league when I'd batted .750 or .800, so he agreed to throw me batting practice one afternoon, and I hit half the balls out of the park but never heard a word about it. Apparently my destiny was to pitch or not to play at all. Which meant that I'd better become a better pitcher in a hurry.

If baseball wasn't fun anymore, why did I still care about playing? And did I really care? Or was it just a lifetime's momentum carrying me from day to day? Those were the riddles I couldn't answer after I left Arizona and drove my red Celica twenty-three hours straight to Brownwood. It was disappointing to discover that the thing you thought you wanted all your life doesn't feel at all the way you thought it was going to feel.

When I reached Brownwood I slept for two days, then took off to see Patricia at Texas A&M in College Station, about five hours southeast. It had been two and a half years since we'd lived in the same town, but nothing had changed between us. Being with her allowed me to pretend I was happy. Too bad I couldn't stay there until spring training.

The first week I was home I helped Mom carry Kael in from the car. He was all but unconscious and wrapped in a brown Hefty bag. At lunch he'd downed a bottle of cherry vodka and puked and pooped all over himself in class. He was in the eighth grade, only fifteen. Mom cried and explained that he'd fallen in with a bad crowd and was probably doing other drugs besides alcohol. She said she blamed herself and Dad.

"Maybe we were too hard on you," she said. "But we were too lenient with Kael. That boy is lost, and I don't know what to do."

I wished I could help, but my brother and I lived in separate worlds. In a lot of ways he'd become the anti-Jimmy, choosing his path because it led in the opposite direction from mine. No words that came from my mouth would have any impact. Besides, I wasn't doing so swell myself.

Dad worked days at Ernest's store, trying with his brother Bob to keep it alive. That took a lot of his time (and ultimately proved futile), and when he and then Mom came home in the evenings I usually left to jog through the dark streets in order not to breathe the toxic air between them; they hated each other by then.

It's cool in the fall and winter, and I could run for hours. I was alone and it felt right. The long miles helped to clear my mind of trash thoughts, and my absence from baseball seemed to rekindle my love for it. Baseball was a game, that's all; a game I'd loved all my life. I kept reminding myself of that, and within a few weeks I found myself looking for someone to play catch with. I asked Dad. He found a catcher's mitt and crouched down in the backyard. I threw a fastball that popped the leather so hard it sounded like a shotgun blast. "That's enough," Dad said, shaking his hand. He dropped the glove and walked in the house.

Topic one of conversation among minor leaguers, especially those in single-A ball, is age—trying to guess that mysterious and unknowable number at which a prospect suddenly reaches has-beenhood in the organization's eyes. "Man, if you're not at the big show by the time you're [fill in the blank], you're done." Most guys figured twenty-six as the magic year. We were all racing the calendar.

Conversations like those, I was pleased to note, no longer put the fear of damnation into me. That first year of pro ball had been a great education. I'd learned that baseball is as much business as game, but it still has to be played. I'd lived through the worst and believed I understood how to run the minefield without blowing myself up. You do it by paying more attention to where you are than to where you're going, no matter how distracting your dream is as it sits on the horizon, nearly close enough to touch. I was only twenty. All I had to do was progress a little every year, beginning this year by making the low-A team in Beloit, Wisconsin. It was a modest goal, and spring training became a giddy time. I went about playing with the attitude that nothing could surprise me now.

Then I met Alfredo, a pitcher from the Dominican Republic. He'd missed the previous season with an arm injury but worked hard in the off-season and said he expected to make at least Beloit, if not the high-A team in Stockton, California. He looked good enough to do it, too, and I was happy for him, not jealous, when he pitched well in his first outing. If nothing else he showed that his arm was healthy.

By the time we filed into the locker room after the game, Alfredo's locker had been cleaned out and a plane ticket placed on his gear. Boom, just like that. He was being released. Why? For whatever reason, the Brewers had lost interest. Maybe they thought his arm was suspect now and preferred not to take a chance on him. They hadn't released him before because rules stated that players couldn't be cut as long as they were hurt. Once he showed he'd healed, they jumped on the chance.

What a cold-blooded way to tell him. You should've seen his face. I still can. It was one of those moments. They'd destroyed a man's lifetime dream, acting like slaughterhouse butchers. We weren't even human.

Team assignments were posted at the end of spring training and I made the low-A team in Beloit, a town of thirty thousand or so on the Wisconsin-Illinois border, twenty miles above Rockford. I read that the great anthropologist Margaret Mead once called Beloit "a microcosm of America." What she was doing in Beloit, instead of in Samoa or New Guinea, I don't know, but the town hardly mimicked my American experiences. These northern people were colder, more distant, and ruder than people in the South. I felt like a stranger among them. Of course, I was miserable anyway, living in a trailer with pitcher Dave Stapleton and his wife. They were devoutly religious and always trying to dissuade me from my sinning ways. If I went out with teammates after a game for a few beers, they would wait up for me and offer biblical counsel.

"You need to read the Book," Dave would say.

Well, I did read the Bible. I just didn't see the verses prohibiting a young man from blowing off a little steam and having a few laughs and trying to make some friends. Didn't Scripture recommend "taking a little wine for thy stomach's sake"?

At least once a day Dave told me I was destined for hell. And at least once a day I wanted to tell him I was already there.

Calling home for moral support was not an option. Mom and Dad were suffering with each other, one of them always moving out or threatening to, and Kael was still drinking and doing drugs. They all had bigger problems to deal with than my insecurities.

The best three days of that summer were when Patricia and her parents drove up on vacation. She'd just graduated college. They came to games all three days, and I pitched one of them and won, probably because I felt so relaxed having them there. After that game Patricia walked back toward the fieldhouse with me. Mike Birkbeck, a pitcher on our team with a wicked curveball, ran up and introduced himself. He stared at her for a moment, smiling, probably not believing that I had such a great-looking girlfriend.

"You're in over your head," he said to me.

I don't remember much about that year after Patricia left. Even winning the league championship (we had a lot of the same players, and the same manager in Tom Gamboa, as the rookie team) didn't stick in my brain. My record was nine and ten, with an ERA of five-something. It was better than the previous season, but it wasn't good.

The following year they sent me back to Beloit after spring training. Most of my old teammates had moved up to at least the organization's high-A team in Stockton, where Tom was the new manager. I didn't take the news well that I wouldn't be with them. But at least I was designated the number one starter.

Something told me I wouldn't be long for Beloit. My sense was that with a good showing on opening day I'd be Stockton-bound by the next day. But even if I didn't show well, I'd probably be sent up. Isn't that what always happened when I made a close friend? Weren't we always separated soon enough?

Gary Kanwisher was a big, muscular kid from New

Jersey with thick brown hair, a friendly smile, and an easy manner. He'd just pitched for Oklahoma State in the College World Series, and I liked him more than anyone I'd met in a long time. We bonded like soldiers in a foxhole and found an apartment together. He said the way we talked till 3 A.M. reminded him of being a freshman in the dorm. I said it didn't remind me of anything I'd ever done, and told him that Dad had raised me to be seen and not heard.

The night before opening day Gary and I went out to eat at Cheers, a restaurant-bar in Beloit. I polished off a hamburger, a Coke, and some nachos, and went home to get eight hours' sleep. When the pain woke me at two in the morning, I thought I had food poisoning or a stomach virus. So why wasn't I throwing up? And why did it hurt so much? I curled up on the bathroom floor and clutched my stomach and moaned until four, then yelled for Gary to fetch Pete Kolb, the team's trainer.

Pete drove me to the hospital. The doctor said my appendix was about to burst. I asked if I'd be well enough to pitch in a few hours. A nurse came in and gave me a shot, and the next thing I remember is waking up in the recovery room without my appendix. The doctor said it would be at least four weeks until I could play again. Gary promised he'd take good care of me when they weren't on the road. But my first night out of the hospital he dragged me to a working-class bar

that was two-deep in guys wearing T-shirts and jeans.
I painfully lowered myself onto a stool in the corner.
Gary went to get himself a beer and me some juice.

I didn't see what started it, but within a minute the
place was brawling, like Saturday night in an Old West
saloon—punches landed, furniture thrown, glassware
shattering, blood spurting, bodies flying. I looked
around for Gary. He'd been swallowed by the melee.
Not for a second did I consider joining in. Whom
would I hit and why? Besides, I had that hole in my
side; I imagined someone's foot going right through it
and out the back. The front door was thirty feet and
five fights too far to reach safely, so I slid off my stool
and hid under the table. When there were more guys
lying on the floor than standing, Gary grabbed me by
the neck and pulled me out. He'd been hiding, too. We
laughed all night and agreed that the North wasn't
very civilized.

A few days later Gary and I played catch outside
our apartment building. Pete happened to drive by and
told management. I was sent home to Texas with an
edict to do absolutely nothing. By the time I got back
to Beloit, the season was two months old and the clock
on my career was ticking fast.

Coach told me I'd be pitching only one inning my
first game back, a game we were losing when I came in
to mop up in the ninth. I struck out two of the batters
and retired the third on a pop-up. In the bottom of the

inning we tied the score, so I stayed in and pitched an easy tenth. By the time we won the game in the eleventh I'd pitched three innings and had four strike-outs with no hits and no walks. The hardest hit ball was an eight-hopper to the shortstop. I felt right again, back on track for the future. To celebrate, Gary and I drove to a bar in Rockford and got in after two. The phone was ringing.

"Where the hell you been?" the manager said. "I've been calling all night. Pack your stuff. You need to be at O'Hare Airport in Chicago at ten. You're moving up to Stockton."

I sat on the plane for California thinking about how you should be careful what you wish for. Gary was someone I'd known for only a few months and yet felt closer to than anyone except Patricia—but no matter how much I thought I loved her, I had to admit that time and distance and opposite paths left us no future; you can't build a romance or marriage on letters and phone calls. And you can't build friendships in baseball.

Gary was the childhood friend I'd never made. He lifted me out of Jimmy's World and made me laugh, and the best I could hope for was his promotion to Stockton or wherever else I might be playing. A voice inside hissed that that was a long shot. And as I sat there eating peanuts and drinking Cokes, it occurred to me that I was all but alone in the world and would stay that way until I made the major leagues and lasted in one place long enough to unpack my suitcase and hang some art. This was my life. I'd spent the first twenty-one years waiting for it to begin, it hadn't started yet, and I wouldn't have known how to change it even if I wanted. You'd never have guessed, looking at my face from across the aisle, that this plane was carrying me one step closer to my lifelong dream. And it was a giant step, too. I closed my eyes and tried to sleep for the first time in thirty hours. No chance.

They call Stockton the "All-America City." I saw the words written on the city limits sign and wondered what Margaret Mead would have to say about that. My experience was that Stockton and Beloit shared a lot of grumpy people. Not a "yes, ma'am" or a "no, sir" in earshot.

Stockton is about a hundred miles dead east of San Francisco, so it does have the right geographical latitude. It's the longitude that leaves something to be desired. California's interior reminds you of West Texas in how desolate it can be. Even after a rain it looks parched. My first afternoon there I lay by the pool at my motel under the hot sun and found myself covered in ashes from fires burning hundreds of miles away.

It was good to see Tom Gamboa, the manager, and some of the other guys I'd played with for two years. I made my first start, pitching six shutout innings for the win, and five days after that I went seven innings, allowing a single run. I was doing better than Dan Plesac and heard rumors about possibly being sent up to double-A if my next outing was as good as my first two.

The difference in me was all mental. For whatever reason I strode to the mound as if I owned the batters. It wasn't a question of what they might do to my pitches but what I was going to do to their bats. I pictured the ball flying out of my hand like a little Stealth bomber that could avoid the bat's radar.

The confidence went to my head. I let fantasies get the best of me, picturing myself in a Brewers uniform, signing autographs for kids and going out with the team for some beer and sauerbraten in downtown Milwaukee after my no-hitter.

My third game was terrible, and then things got worse. It was as though I'd fallen into a bottomless pit; I kept falling. I didn't stride to the mound as much as tiptoe out there, and instead of pitching I wished the ball to the plate, praying that the batter would make a mistake. Again, the difference was all mental. In place of confidence was the kind of self-doubt that wraps its fingers around your neck. I counted down the days between starts—four, three, two, one—with a dread usually reserved for funerals and root canals. Four losses later I told the coaching staff that I would prefer to be a relief pitcher. My mental makeup, I said, was better suited to that role; I hated knowing ahead of time which day I would be pitching, and then if I pitched poorly I'd have four days to brood about the past and fear the future.

It was a good story and the truth, but not the whole truth. The part I left out was that my arm felt chronically sore, too sore to launch 110 pitches a game. Why didn't I tell them? Fear. The fear they might think of me as a wuss, the way Gordon Wood had when I separated my shoulder. "You've gotta be able to tell the difference between soreness and pain," the coaches told pitchers. "A little soreness is normal." Well, hell, how was I supposed to know the difference? It depended on your pain threshold, and mine was pretty high. Between soreness and pain, I decided to err on the side of Texas football. So I said nothing.

I wasn't just the team's weak link. I was its black hole. The best I can say of those times is that I didn't commit suicide. And I didn't only because I threw just well enough now and then to have hope. What stands out most in memory is a game we played against Mark McGwire's team in Modesto. Everyone already knew about Mark's potential, and early in the game he added to the buzz by hitting a rocket off of Jeff Parrett that would have cleared the stadium if the scoreboard in left-center had been just a few feet shorter. No one wanted to pitch to him, so when he came up later in the game with the bases loaded and Tom called me in from the bull pen, I groaned. I couldn't remember ever giving up a grand slam, but the possibility was vivid in my brain as soon as I took the mound and saw how huge he was. I'd never seen a bigger baseball player. He looked like Paul Bunyan. Two of my forearms equaled half of his. If he swung with one hand, he'd still hit thirty homers.

I figured I had nothing to lose and let fly with a fastball that shot fire through my elbow. Swing and a miss. Second pitch the same; it hurt but was a strike. Third pitch broke over the plate and he never moved. Called strike three.

Of course, he wasn't yet the Mark McGwire who hit seventy home runs in one major-league season, so my moment of triumph wasn't much more than a short-lived moral victory and a tease about what might be and could be if only I learned how to control my pitches and temper, and tell the difference between soreness and pain. I finished the season with five wins against six losses, a crummy 6.04 ERA, and a gnawing ache in my elbow.

The Brewers sent me back to the fall instructional league, and I pitched several more painful innings. One morning I woke with my left arm locked from forearm to biceps. A huge knot had appeared above the elbow and discolored the area a grotesque purple. Nothing could budge it. Dan Plesac, my dorm roommate, used both hands to try straightening it. He strained and groaned but it was as obstinate as a frozen lug nut.

The doctor said, "It's tendinitis."

Tendinitis? Tendinitis didn't hurt this much, and besides, who'd ever heard of tendinitis locking your arm?

Apparently the Brewers had, because they kept me in Arizona to ice it, heat it, and exercise it until the league ended in October, then sent me to orthopedic surgeon Frank Jobe, in Los Angeles. He examined the elbow and sent me home with instructions to keep up the routine until spring training in February, but to come back and see him at the end of November if it hadn't healed by then. By the time I reached Brownwood, I'd decided that the best therapy I could give my elbow would be to forget about baseball and get a real job for a while. I needed to grow up more than I needed to pitch.

CHAPTER FIVE

IT WAS 1958, the year of Khrushchev, the four-cent stamp, and the Dodgers' leaving Brooklyn. It was the year Vera Cloud married Vernon Eakin.

Vera was thirty-two and widowed with four children. Vernon was forty-five and divorced with four children. They lived in the Central Texas town of Killeen, next to Fort Hood, which Texans are proud to point out is the free world's largest military base. Vera had been a teacher, but Vernon didn't want her to work. She got pregnant and had a miscarriage, then got pregnant again, and in 1962, at the risk of her life, gave birth to a beautiful girl with dark hair and darker eyes. This would be the only child they conceived together, so Vernon and Vera christened their daughter

Verna, a blending of the two names, but Verna grew to hate her name; if you didn't want a black eye, you called her Lorri.

The Cold War that kept Fort Hood growing was good for Killeen and for contractors like Vernon. People needed homes, and more people needed more homes, and in 1963 Vernon was able to build his family a dream home and cattle ranch just outside Nolanville, twenty minutes away. It was in an area that had been an early white settlement a hundred years before, on land in the middle of nowhere, with a population counted in the dozens. But Vernon envisioned more than just miles of nothing. He envisioned hundreds of neighbors and began building some of their houses. Others built more houses, strangers came to buy them, and the town Vernon had imagined came to life.

Lorri and Nolanville grew together. The town now had three churches, an elementary school, a volunteer fire department, and a convenience store. Lorri was tall and pretty and smart and her father's favorite. Every day she passed by the street that he'd named for her. She was too young to understand why her older sisters seemed so anxious to leave the nest. Then she began to notice how Daddy acted toward Mommy. So Lorri started to drift away from him a little. Her mother went back to teaching and taught Lorri that young women need to be independent.

"Get an education. Get a skill," Vera said. "Then no

matter what happens, you know you can rely on yourself."

One day Vernon fell on a job site and broke his arm. It seemed to heal badly, and for a year the hospital treated the arthritis that doctors thought he had until tests discovered bone cancer. Vernon was dying.

Lorri graduated high school in 1980 and didn't attend the prom because her boyfriend was the Baptist pastor's son and didn't dance.

One night Lorri called home and asked her mother if she could stay out with some of her friends from junior college. Mom said no.

"Please, Mama," Lorri said. "I don't ever do anything. I always work when I get home. Please."

"Let me ask your daddy," Vera said, putting down the phone and then coming back. "He said no, he wants you to come home."

Lorri was furious. "I'm nineteen years old," she shouted. "I'm in college, I'm working, and I'm going to the movies tonight with my friends." And she hung up.

She came home late from seeing *Chariots of Fire*, about a Christian Olympic sprinter, and found that Daddy had had a spell. Vernon never did regain full consciousness and died in the hospital two weeks later.

Lorri blamed herself and didn't cry at the funeral. After the dry wake she drove straight to her biology lab class and apologized to the teacher for being late. It would take a long time for Lorri to stop feeling guilty and to cry tears of grief.

Vernon's medical expenses had eaten much of the family's wealth, and most of what should have been left was missing. The only one who knew what had happened to all the money was dead.

All of Lorri's brothers and sisters were married. If she went off to college, her mother would be alone. But Vera insisted, and Lorri applied for scholarships and financial aid. Before starting Howard Payne University, she spent the summer working at a Baptist conference center in Glorieta, New Mexico. It was her first time away from home, and at twenty-three she loved making her own decisions. When the fall semester began, she changed her major from psychology to business.

Howard Payne University has a student body of fifteen hundred, on a pleasant campus in the middle of Brownwood. It was founded in 1889 by the Pecan Valley Baptist Association as a Christian liberal arts school after a local pastor secured an endowment from his wealthy brother-in-law, Edward Howard Payne. (Edward, like Lorri, preferred his middle name.) It's known as a school for future pastors and future pastors' wives.

Lorri dated a little, not much. She studied too hard to have the time, and anyway had to work as a bank teller at a drive-through window.

Before her final semester in the fall of 1985, Lorri found a part-time job filing papers and giving campus tours in the Howard Payne admissions office. When a full-time secretary's job opened up, Lorri called Pam

Messer, a married woman she'd worked with at the bank. Pam hated being a drive-through teller and applied for and got the secretary's job, and the two women continued their friendship. Lorri told Pam that she'd stopped dating; all she cared about was finishing school with good grades and putting herself in a good position for grad school. She laughed about the single date she'd had with a baseball player, some egotistical jerk who talked all night about how great a pitcher he was and who couldn't pass a mirror or window reflection without stopping to admire himself.

"Every baseball player I've ever met is like that," she declared. "I will never go out with another baseball player as long as I live."

I told Mom I needed a job until spring training began, and she said the Brownwood site of the state correctional facility for juvenile delinquents had an opening for a recreation assistant. The rec director was Wade Messer, a ministerial student at HPU who thought of the inmates as souls waiting to be saved. You'd have to see these kids to appreciate Wade's idealism. They weren't in for stealing hubcaps and toilet-papering a neighbor's pecan tree. Some of them were murderers, rapists, and armed robbers. One little kid with wide eyes and a bright smile had been inspired by a slasher movie to shoot up the local mall with his daddy's gun. Wade ran recreation programs for them that rewarded good behavior. He needed some help. I applied and he hired me on the spot.

The state facility is a large complex surrounded by a fourteen-foot fence, on the city's southwest corner. On one side is a residential area; the other backs up to rattlesnake fields bisected by a Santa Fe railroad track. Sometimes when kids escaped they'd break for the tracks and hope to jump a freedom train. School personnel would fan out across town on foot or in vans with radios or police scanners and corner them and bring them back in handcuffs. The directors sent me out to help because they believed the kids liked me and wouldn't try to hurt me if I was alone with them. Besides, I was a lot faster than anyone else. I'd run through the fields in shorts with my walkie-talkie, hoping to find the kid before I saw a snake.

You have to prove yourself to these kids, who'd just as soon stick a knife in your leg as trust you. They all have stories that break your heart and come from families that aren't. I remember a Houston kid, fourteen years old and in trouble for cutting a schoolmate. Turned out his father came home a few times a week, handcuffed him to the bed, and sodomized him. The handcuffs were Dad's from work; he was a cop.

I'd hear these stories and love my own parents and think, *There but for the grace of God*. I earned trust by treating the kids with respect. I called all of them "ma'am" and "sir." It wasn't phony and they knew it. I listened when they talked and talked less than listened. They appreciated that.

The boys also liked the way I played basketball. Even with a sore elbow, I was better than they were. In that way the state school was a lot like a playground. The better athlete you were, the more they admired you.

My manner and skills made me a natural mediator. Kids came to me for advice and turned themselves over to my custody after they did something stupid, something deserving of punishment. I put my arm around a lot of shoulders and made a lot of little speeches encouraging them to trust the adults in charge instead of treating them like the enemy.

"They're only trying to help you do your time and get better and get back home and go on with your life," I said. "You have to take your punishment now for what you did, but you can make it easy on yourself from now on."

Wade had formed a basketball team as an incentive program. The kids who'd earned the right through sustained good behavior got to travel around the area, playing teams from regular schools. The idea worked; no one wanted to lose such a great perk. Wade coached, and I was his assistant. We watched bad kids go good and saw every one of them trying to be a team player. Winning or losing didn't matter; this was all winning. Wade and I became friends, and he said he didn't look forward to losing me in February, but he sure understood the need to chase dreams. He'd done the same thing a few years before, when he went back to school in his midtwenties and fulfilled a lifelong ambition by beginning to work on his divinity degree. He dreamed of being a pastor and leading his own congregation.

One day Wade asked if I wanted to meet a young woman he knew, a graduating senior who worked with his wife in the admissions office at Howard Payne. Her name was Lorri. He described her as pretty, smart, and fun. I said what the hell, and Wade said he'd set up the rendezvous.

The plan was for Wade, his wife Pam, and I to go to HPU's football game, at Gordon Wood Stadium, that Saturday, and I could see Lorri before meeting her. "She'll be on the sidelines," he said.

Wow, a cheerleader, I thought. "She must be pretty good-looking," I said.

At the game I studied all the cheerleaders, picked my two or three favorites, and asked Wade which one Lorri was.

"She's right there," he said, pointing to someone pretending to fly around, in a huge yellow-jacket costume.

"Go, Yellow Jackets," the cheerleaders yelled.

"Wait a second," I said. "You mean she's the mascot?"

"Yep," Wade said. He waved at Lorri until he got her attention. She waved back and continued with her routine. For all I knew she looked like the Bride of Frankenstein underneath that costume. It did impress me, though, that she kept her energy up in the heat that had to feel twice as hot under all that polyester.

We were supposed to meet right after the game but Lorri didn't want anyone to see her until she'd showered and put on fresh makeup. I went with Wade and Pam to their house, which happened to be my grandparents' old house that was sold after Ernest died; the new owner had rented it out. I knew every inch of that place. Maybe that's why I was so relaxed when Lorri came in.

I thought she was beautiful—tall, with long, wavy hair, dark eyes, and a big smile—just the way Wade described her.

We played a card game, Uno, that she'd never played, and I saw she wasn't catching on to the strategy of whether to throw a wild card or match the color in order to get rid of her cards first, which is the game's object. I beat her every hand and ribbed her. She took it good-naturedly and joked back.

"If you're trying to make a good impression, you're not doing it the right way," she said after losing another game. But she was smiling when she said it.

There was an easy rapport between us. I couldn't help noticing that she was the first woman since Patricia with whom I'd had any real rapport. I was comfortable and she was comfortable. Imagine that. This time my being quiet was an asset. She asked me a little about baseball and I wasn't in the mood to say too much about it; I was more interested in hearing what she did and wanted out of life, and that impressed her. Given the last dating experience she'd had with a ballplayer, I don't know why she decided to take a chance on me. And she doesn't either, other than to explain that she makes a lot of decisions by gut instinct. She walked in prepared to listen to me talk about myself all night. Instead I made her laugh and smoked her in cards. I'm a competitive SOB, even if I am trying to impress a girl. She liked that I didn't patronize her.

I drove her home and she asked me to church the next morning. She knew I was Methodist, not Baptist, but I said fine. Her Baptist church was right across the street from Howard Payne. It had been a while since I'd been to services, and I thought the Baptist services were just different enough to seem new and interesting. Afterward we promenaded around a city park and sat on a bench in a gazebo. If opposites attract, then we were a heavenly match. Lorri loved to talk. She told me about the gag questionnaire she and her sorority sisters had devised, "101 Easy-Answer Essay Questions to Ask a Guy Before Going Out with Him." Every girl came up with her most shallow prerequisites for dating; they called it the "No Data Beta." Lorri's guy had to be tall, dark-haired, and have either a mustache or the potential to grow one.

"Would you mind growing a mustache?" she asked me.

I laughed and took it as a good sign.

We saw each other every weekend and in the days between I thought about her all the time. Her image went with me to the correctional school and made the pain in my elbow more tolerable. I took her home to meet my parents, and Mom brought out the baby pictures. Lorri's face said this was too much, too soon. But I began growing a mustache.

One night we had a fight over religion, and she stormed out of the car. "I am never marrying someone who isn't a Baptist," she shouted, slamming the door and running into her dorm room.

The next day she called to apologize. She said true faith wasn't about being Baptist or Methodist or Hindu; it was about what you did with your faith in the world. And then she came a few times with me to Central Methodist, just to see how the other side lives.

It's fair to say that for all the listening I did and all the talking Lorri did, I knew less about what she wanted from life than she knew about me, not because she listened better or talked worse, but because she hadn't yet narrowed her possibilities. You can't get much simpler than dreaming of playing baseball for twenty years, or more complicated than waking each day without knowing what you want to do. For her the degree meant everything. It would lead her somewhere. She'd already declined a job way down near Corpus Christi, as a caseworker for the South Texas Baptist Children's Home, when one of those mysterious feelings told her she wasn't supposed to be there.

This was Lorri's last semester. Come December, she'd have some decisions to make. It was like a math problem. I watched her trying to solve it and wondered where I fit into the equation. How much did I count for in her life? My personality didn't allow me to come right out and ask; what she said or did would reveal the answer. I was certain where I wanted to go, but it was too soon to say whether I wanted her to go along with me, even if she wanted to. I'd traveled too far to let love get in the way of my dream. Or was that just my fear talking, the fear that she didn't care for me as much as I did for her?

By Thanksgiving, my elbow still hurt. I flew back to Los Angeles for a day and found my way to the Kerlan-Jobe Orthopaedic Clinic.

Doctors Kerlan and Jobe were the first superstars of sports medicine. Robert Kerlan had been in private practice when he was named the Los Angeles Dodgers first team physician in 1958, and he then became either the team physician or consultant to a number of other professional teams. In 1965 he asked Frank Jobe, with whom he'd worked at Los Angeles County General

Hospital, to be his partner. Together and separately they shot orthopedic surgery into the space age by pioneering techniques that then seemed like science fiction. It's hard to remember now how futuristic their work was, and it's impossible to count how many careers they saved. Tommy John's, for example. When Dr. Jobe replaced John's useless elbow tendon with one from his wrist, it was a last-ditch, nothing-to-lose effort and no one realistically expected the pitcher to pitch again. That was 1974. Two years later, Tommy John did come back, and with amazing success. Many others followed. By the time I got to the Kerlan-Jobe Orthopaedic Clinic in the fall of 1985, the two doctors had a reputation for changing the miraculous into the status quo.

Dr. Jobe came in to my exam room. He was distinguished looking, with white hair and a calm manner. The walls were plastered with photos of the athletes he'd operated on. It would've been hard to think of a famous ballplayer who hadn't been his patient. He took my arm and twisted it and turned it and lifted it and bent it and pinched it, and after every new movement he asked, "Does that hurt?" I answered yes and ouch each time.

Dr. Jobe excused himself for a few minutes, then returned and said that we should wait until January; if it hadn't healed by then, and I still wanted to pursue my pitching career, I'd need the "Tommy John surgery" to replace the damaged elbow tendon with one from my wrist. It was still experimental, he warned, and at minimum I'd be unable to throw for a year.

I said that I of course wanted to pitch again and was sure I'd be seeing him in January and wished we could do the surgery right now so that I could get back sooner. Waiting until January would put my career on hold until at least spring training of 1987. He shrugged his shoulders and shook my hand, and I left.

The disappointment hit me like a death in the family. I pouted and wondered why we hadn't done the surgery months before, instead of waiting uselessly. The answer was obvious. Had all things been equal, Dr. Jobe would've wheeled me into the operating room that afternoon. But the Brewers wanted to hold off on spending twenty or thirty grand on the operation until the need was inescapable. They wouldn't have waited a day if the elbow belonged to a superstar like Rollie Fingers, and they'd never spend even a dime on me if they hadn't already made that $35,000 investment. These were the rules of the game.

When my mind moved past all that, only fear remained. What if the surgery wasn't successful? What if I couldn't pitch anymore? And what would I do with myself for a year before finding out?

With Lorri's help, I came up with some answers:

One, the surgery would be successful. Dr. Jobe had pioneered this technique and was learning more each time he performed it.

Two, I would absolutely be able to pitch again, even

if only knuckleballs. "Hey, maybe it'll make me a better pitcher," I said, thinking about God's mysterious ways.

Three, I could continue working at the school for another year. But that meant staying in my parents' house. My paycheck wasn't enough to rent a place of my own, and I'd already spent almost all of my baseball signing bonus making up the difference between what the Brewers paid me during the season and what it cost to live. I'd always considered a few months home in the off-season to be an extended hotel stay. But I couldn't consider fifteen months as anything other than living there.

My future would have seemed less bleak if Lorri had stayed in Brownwood. But when she finished classes in December and lost her scholarship money, she moved to her mom's in Nolanville and found a job working for Rio Delta Airlines, Delta's short-haul carrier in Texas, out of the Killeen airport.

I was lucky that Lorri's graduation ceremony wouldn't be held until May, and she had a final research paper due within the month. She liked the way I wrote and asked me to help. I was glad for any reason to be near her and drove the three hours with a cold so bad, I got more sneezes per mile than miles per gallon. My symptoms worsened the closer I came to Nolanville, which has an absurdly high cedar count that's deadly for people with allergies. By the time I reached Lorri's house, my eyes were swollen shut and my nose was like a faucet—and Lorri wasn't there. Her mom said she'd gone shopping in Killeen and told me I looked terrible and to sit down. She made me some soup and tea and we visited awhile, and the next thing I knew Lorri was waking me up on the couch. We worked on her paper in between my nose-blowings. They were so frequent I ended up jamming a Kleenex in each nostril to stanch the flow. It made Lorri laugh. I loved making her laugh. And I hated leaving to come home.

She got an "A" on the paper.

I called Dr. Jobe's office the first week in January and made an appointment for the surgery. Some days later I flew to Los Angeles and checked into the Kerlan-Jobe clinic, just north of the airport. I closed my eyes and went under the anesthetic believing that I would still be a big-league baseball player and anxious for the next twelve months to pass.

When I opened my eyes in the recovery room, I saw a familiar face, but I was groggy, and it took a few seconds for my eyes to focus.

"Lorri?!"

She was standing over me, stroking my head. "Hey, Jimmy," she said softly.

"What are you doing here?"

"I wanted to be with you."

"How long have you been here?"

"Hours. You've been out cold for a long time. The nurse said they had to knock you silly."

Not even Billy Graham standing by my bed with a Bible would have surprised me more. I was still a little under the influence and thought Lorri looked like a saint from a Renaissance painting—hovering with a white halo.

She grabbed my hand and kissed it. "How do you feel?" she asked.

"Better," I said, trying to smile.

"Does it hurt a lot?" She reached toward my elbow without touching. It was wrapped in bandages and covered with a removable half cast.

But it wasn't my elbow that hurt; it was my ankle, and it was killing me. She explained: The doctors couldn't transplant the tendon from my wrist and had to take one from my ankle instead. It was wrapped thick. I glanced over at the only pair of shoes I'd brought for my two-day clinic trip, a pair of ostrich cowboy boots, and wondered how the hell I was going to get them on.

"I'm glad you came," I said, squeezing her hand. "I'm really glad."

My eyes filled up and I tried not to cry. For months I'd hoped that Lorri cared about me the way I cared for her, and I wondered if she could ever love me, but I'd always pushed those thoughts away; I had to protect myself in case she didn't and couldn't. Now I saw that she could—or maybe did. This was the loudest anyone had ever told me, "I love you."

It took all my strength not to propose marriage right then. That would have been wrong. Even I knew that. Even then.

Lorri spent those four days and three nights on the couch in my room. The nurses brought her blankets and pillows and meals, but she didn't get much sleep. Someone was always coming in to check my vitals and give me painkillers, and I dozed in and out. On the last morning, they changed the wrapping and pinned my elbow to my chest and discharged me, and Lorri helped me get my boots on. We called a cab for the airport ride, and flew to Austin and from there to Killeen. Lorri drove us to her mom's house in Nolanville and put me into her dad's old recliner.

I'd had to raise my pain threshold for the trip, but even with the bar raised high over my head now I wasn't prepared for how excruciating removing my boots would be. Forget the elbow; that felt fine. It was my ankle that made me want to holler. The plane ride and having to sit for eight hours without keeping my leg elevated had swelled it wider than the boots. Lorri and her mom yanked while I gripped the sides of the chair and groaned. Afterward, I thought of those cowboy movies in which the faithful friend uses a hunting knife to remove a bullet from the shoulder of the hero, who keeps himself from screaming by biting on leather.

I knew enough about Lorri to figure out that I

wouldn't have been sitting there, with her waiting on me, if her mother didn't like me.

"Mama, I think it's the real thing," she had told her mother the day I flew to California. "I really love this guy, and I want to be out there with him, for moral support. He needs it."

"Are you sure, really sure?" Vera had asked.

"Yes, Mama. Don't you like him?"

"Very much," she'd said, thinking for a moment and then smiling. "You go on and take care of your man."

I stayed all night in her recliner, watching TV and dozing. In the morning I turned to CNN for coverage of the space shuttle launch. Space flight had interested me since I was first old enough to understand it. I was sorry when they stopped sending astronauts to the moon. I'd liked looking up and imagining that someone was walking there. But the space shuttle seemed more like a ride at Disneyland. You go up, zoom around for a while, and come home. Whatever invisible experiments they did up there weren't as interesting to me as walking around on that big object in the sky. I figured I'd open the windows that night, or even go outside if I felt up to it, and stare up. Maybe I'd see the *Challenger* pass overhead.

And then as I watched, it blew up and became a trail of smoke that lingered and drifted down.

The videotape played over and over. Seventy-three seconds into the flight, a faulty O-ring had begun a chain reaction in the liquid fuel tanks that resulted in an explosion that obliterated seven astronauts. I watched the replays until I was numb. All of those people, including a teacher, suddenly ceased to exist a minute and thirteen seconds after their dream came true. There were no guarantees in life.

I parked in front of Nathan's Jewelers in Brownwood. Did I really want to do this? Yes. I walked in and with help picked out an engagement ring. It cost $2,500—most of what I still had left from my bonus. I drove to Nolanville on Valentine's Day, the most romantic day of the year, and waited until Lorri and I were alone, then waited some more until the mood seemed right. I dropped to one knee in front of the chair and said, "Lorri, I love you and I'd like to spend the rest of my life with you. I hope you feel the same way, and if you do, well, I want you to marry me. Will you? Do you?"

She said, "I do, Jimmy, I really do."

I showed her the ring and she put her arms around my neck and kissed me, and then she told her mother, and in a few days we set a July date.

Lorri had never watched me play baseball, or even throw one. She'd never seen me in uniform. As far as she knew, my dream was a pipe dream. How could she know whether my elbow would heal enough to play again? And if I did play, what were the chances that I'd

make the big leagues and bring home a big-league paycheck? If I didn't, what then? How was I going to make
a living? I didn't have a college degree and we couldn't
afford to send me to earn one if that time came. Lorri
was running on faith alone, putting her trust in me and
in God's will, but her mother was a little concerned. I
couldn't blame her, not after the financial difficulties
Vern had left her with. It must've looked as though her
daughter was marrying a man without prospects. And
still she tried to do everything she could to help us.

We said we planned to live in Brownwood, and Vera
bought a small house—two bedrooms with a garage
that could be converted into one—for us to live in; we
would pay just enough rent to cover her mortgage payments. Lorri insisted that we remodel it, and we spent
a lot of money we didn't have on carpentry, painting,
carpeting, new fixtures for the kitchen and bathrooms,
new appliances, and furniture. I had to raise the spending limits on my credit cards to afford everything. The
project seemed to take on a life of its own, getting bigger and bigger. So did the wedding. Lorri and her mom
planned everything; no detail was too small or too ex-
pensive. It was clear that we would be starting our
married life up to our knees in debt.

I worked at the state school and lived at home and
had unlimited energy to exercise my elbow. I was ob-
sessed with getting back sooner than predicted. I figured that if the standard rehab regime put me back on
the field in a year, doing twice the prescribed amount

would get me back in half that time. I had to. Mom and Dad looked as if they were teetering on the brink of murder-suicide, and Kael was throwing his life away in drugs, drink, and trouble, so our house made the state school seem like Mr. Rogers' Neighborhood. At the same time, the wedding had begun to feel more important than the relationship itself, and there was no escaping the pressure anywhere but in the gym. My left elbow was my whole life.

Then, five weeks before the wedding, my parents announced that they were breaking up for good. Mom moved out of the house and into her own place, and filed for divorce.

I should have been thrilled or at least relieved, but I didn't know what I felt or how to describe my confusion or even whom to talk to if I did. All my life I'd carried the burden of a relationship that had poisoned the two people in it and damaged the two sons that it had brought into the world. I bore that responsibility; they'd said so themselves on those nights when they blamed my birth for the misery of being married to each other. Now they were splitting up, and I was to be married. I'd just turned twenty-two. Something felt wrong, and everything seemed overwhelming. Whenever I saw Lorri I sensed the shotgun at my head no less than my parents had after Mom got pregnant. She asked why I seemed distant. I didn't answer and she asked again, then again and again and again.

At last the words tumbled out—fears, doubts, uncertainties—and we talked a long time. I never actually said I didn't want to marry her; I said that I wasn't really sure about the timing or why we were spending so much money we didn't have. I only knew that I loved her and I hoped I wouldn't ever lose her. Lorri gave me back the ring and had the last word.

She said, "If you're not sure, well then let's just cut it off right now, because when I say 'I do,' it's forever. And I'm not going ahead until you feel sure. If it's meant to happen, then it will. In the meantime, I have to go on with my life."

I tried to go on with my life, too. I worked and worked out. It was easier not to miss Lorri during workouts. I began by playing basketball. Shooting and following through seemed to improve my range of motion. I played point guard on an otherwise all-black team that took second place in a state tournament.

My arm felt better every day. In time I played catch with some local kids, and when that felt good after a few times I threw harder, and when that felt good after a few times I called the Brewers to say I thought I might be able to come back before the end of the season. They told me not to rush things.

Lorri had graduated with her class in May and been offered a full-time position in Howard Payne's admissions office. She moved into the finished house we were supposed to live in together. I suffered every time I passed by, or when we met for a walk or dinner. She was angry, and accused me of breaking off the engagement because I was seeing other women.

Mom and I went to dinner at Red Lobster one night. She was a different person away from Dad. Her eyes sparkled again.

On the way home we passed the Nissan car lot. My eye fell on a brand-new red 300ZX. And I wanted it. We went in to talk to the salesman.

I was so full of it. Here I'd gotten all over Lorri for spending money on stuff she liked, but now I wanted to spend $37,000 on another car. And by "another" car I don't mean a different one from the Celica; I mean a different one from the fully equipped Chevy Blazer that had cost me $25,000 four months before—about the time I'd begun worrying whether the wedding was getting us too far in debt.

The salesman came over to talk. He was a big man, in his early fifties, a few years older than Mom. He walked erect, like career military, and shook my hand and Mom's hand and introduced himself as Charles Hale. He seemed trustworthy, as all good salesmen do.

I said, "I'd like that car there," and pointed to the ZX.

"It's a beautiful piece of machinery," he agreed.

"And I'd like payments of $250 a month," I said.

He said, "Everyone wants payments of $250 a month. Do you have something to put down?"

I showed him my Blazer and its payment book, and

he invited us in to the office while he consulted a periodical and made a phone call. When he hung up he said, "I have to tell you that you owe more on this car than I can get out of it. You're upside down, as we say. I don't want to trick you, Mr. Morris. I don't want you to get in over your head. But if you still want that Nissan out there, I'll do everything in my power to help you. Why don't you just think about it for a couple of days, and if you decide to try for the Nissan, you call me back and we'll see what we can do. Don't even drive it, 'cause it may sway you the wrong way. Here, here's my card."

Charles was right. I came to my senses and didn't call him back. But Mom did, a few days later. She asked if he remembered her, and he asked how her son was, and she said, "I guess you do remember me."

"Yes, ma'am."

"I've got a question for you," she said. "Are you always that honest?"

"I try to be," he said. "That way I don't have to remember what lie I told who."

Charles was divorced. His wife of twenty-eight years had walked away a year and a half before. He didn't like alcohol and had three grown children. Mom invited him on a date that Saturday night, but he had a "previous commitment." With a sincere "I'd love to meet you," he invited her to the Ponderosa Ballroom in Abilene, an hour and a half northwest of Brownwood, to dance that Wednesday night. Mom showed up and their eyes locked on each other across the crowded room and they danced. They were married the following year and have had happiness ever since.

Those days were a lesson in irony. It was on Valentine's Day that I'd proposed to Lorri, and I was engaged while Mom and Dad divorced; as soon as I separated from Lorri, Mom got engaged. She was married on Valentine's Day, the date Charles had picked.

By the fall I was desperate to be anywhere but Brownwood. I drove down to San Antonio to see Dr. William Rockwood, an associate of Dr. Jobe. He gave me the green light and I showed up in Arizona for the annual instructional league. People called me "bionic" and "The Six-Million-Dollar Man." I said no, just thirty-five thousand. I threw well, with an ERA in the low threes, and was all but told that if I kept it up I'd begin the following season in Stockton and possibly be moved up to double-A—and then, who knows. Those were the words I needed to hear. The Brewers' staff warned me not to overdo it now. They knew I would, and of course I did.

A week before the fall league ended, my elbow felt as though it had been tortured on the rack. I was despondent. How many more setbacks could I take before I had to admit finally that my dream was a nightmare? But tests showed that the pain was only scar tissue breaking up; nothing to worry about. That made it easy to ignore the pain.

I went back to Brownwood with hopes high again. There wasn't an elbow exercise in the world that I didn't do as I counted the days to spring training.

Lorri and I saw each other now and then, then here and there, then here and now. She'd figured out that I hadn't been dating anyone else, and her guard let down a little; she hadn't, either. The anger was mostly gone. So was my resentment. Something I couldn't see or explain began pulling us together. We anchored each other to reality. If there'd been another week or two before spring training, I might've gotten back down on one knee again and asked for her forgiveness and her hand.

Lorri drove me to Abilene for my flight to Arizona. I gave all my gear to the agent, and Lorri walked me to the gate. I had five minutes before boarding. We turned to each other and stared. Lorri's eyes filled with tears. I rested my hands on her shoulders, and our foreheads came together in weariness and regret and happiness.

"I guess I won't see you for a while," I whispered.

"No, I guess not," she said.

"There's something I need to know, before I get on."

"What, Jimmy?"

"Will you marry me?"

Lorri leaned back, looked startled for a second, then grabbed my neck and hugged.

"Yes," she shrieked. "Yes, of course I will!"

I hugged her harder and reached into my pocket. "This is for you," I said, handing her the engagement ring. "I never brought it back."

There was a minute left before the plane took off. We set a September wedding date.

Some years ago I imagined my life as a seesaw competition between me and some faceless sadist. Each time it was my turn to ride high, he would suddenly jump off the seat and let me plummet.

I breezed through spring training with the best stuff I'd ever had and excellent control; all the pieces came together. So of course when I got to Stockton and was pitching great, I blew out my shoulder. The game was in Bakersfield, an hour and a half outside Los Angeles. I wound up, and as my arm approached the release point, it froze. The ball flew out of my hand and sailed high over the plate, hitting the left edge of the backstop about twenty feet up. I grabbed my shoulder and knew right away it was serious. Dave Machemar, the manager, came running. There was no need to. I walked right past him, off the field and into the clubhouse. More angry and disgusted than hurt, I threw my glove against the wall.

All of that work for nothing. I'd concentrated so hard on the elbow, I had forgotten that my arm had other moving parts. So did the Brewers. They weren't a weightlifting team then; didn't believe in it. We'd run to get in shape and do martial arts for balance. You'd have thought we were moron flamingoes to see us standing in the infield on one leg.

Four years. Four years I'd been in professional baseball, and all I had to show for it was a forehead lined in frustration and a scar on my elbow that was sure to have a neighbor a few inches higher as soon as the doctor saw it.

I drove down to Los Angeles to let Dr. Jobe examine the shoulder. He said he'd have to operate and I'd be out the rest of the season. We set a time for the next morning, and I called Lorri. "Guess what," I said.

She guessed. Took her about three seconds. "Oh, Jimmy," she said. "I'm sorry."

She flew out to be with me that afternoon. We checked into a hotel near the clinic, and Lorri dropped me off at Dr. Jobe's the next morning. Jobe tightened my shoulder, and she picked me up by noon.

"Let's go to the Grand Canyon on the way home," she said.

She was cheery, trying to stay up for me. I was dirty from not showering and groggy and in pain, swallowing pills as if they were Tic-Tacs. You can imagine how much I wanted to talk.

That was all right with Lorri. She did most of the talking anyway. I suppose she didn't want me to sit there and brood, and she knew that if I did I'd end up in a world of my own, two feet but ten light-years away from her. As long as she kept me occupied, I wouldn't think about being disappointed, or wonder why I was being tested this way, or hate God, or cry about how unfair it was that I couldn't catch a break while guys who came in loaded every night on cocaine and Southern Comfort after sleeping with two girls were throwing shutouts and making it to the bigs.

We got out of the car in the Grand Canyon parking lot and walked down to the vista point. "Oh, it's so gorgeous," Lorri said. "Isn't it?"

The right answer was yes—yes, so we could get back in the car. But beauty—even America's greatest natural wonder—is tough to appreciate when all you can see is the film that forms on your eyes from excruciating pain. "Yeah," I said, without enthusiasm.

"Jimmy, I know it hurts you," she said. "I know a lot of things hurt you. But you may never get to see this again. I don't want you to miss it. I want you to put it in your memory and save it."

It was the perfect moment. I stared at Lorri and fell in love with her all over again. This was my life, I realized. I'd spent it always going somewhere without ever really being anywhere. I was twenty-three and had been chasing a dream for twenty years. The world had about as much reality as a dream does a minute after waking.

I inhaled the May air and let it fill my lungs as I

stared down into the canyon. "It's beautiful," I said. "It really is."

Lorri kissed me. We drove away and began talking. I said I was sick of this crap, sick of being disappointed. It was time to start considering alternatives.

Not in my conscious mind but somewhere in my subconscious I realized that I needed a college degree, and that the long journey to graduation began with a single class. I rearranged my hours at the state school and enrolled in Anatomy 101 at Howard Payne. I loved science—meaning that of all the classes I didn't pay attention to in school, I'd ignored science the least. Besides, I already had a head start on anatomy by knowing the arm so well.

What surprised me wasn't that I got a higher grade than my pre-med classmates; it was that I enjoyed learning and actually learned. Everything the professor said and the textbook explained made sense. Every bone and organ had its place, and I could put them all in it. I found pleasure in just sitting quietly and knowing something new, something that felt useful in the real world, and I finally understood why people say knowledge is power.

Out of nowhere, another job fell in my lap when Tres Womack heard through Lorri that I was in town. Tres and I knew each other from summer-league baseball. He'd been given the job of founding Howard Payne's baseball program, which the school had never had but which its president, who was somehow related to Tres, wanted. Since you can't start a program without players, Tres needed to recruit and audition them, and he asked me to help him judge talent. We went to an open major-league tryout camp in Killeen and wrote down the names and numbers of some kids who were good but not good enough to get the scouts' attention, then we came home and called them and held our own tryouts. We met other kids through these kids and offered scholarships and half scholarships and pretty soon we had a team. It wasn't going to win any championships right away, but it was a start. And I loved the work. I realized that as long as I could be near baseball, I'd probably be okay. Life goes on, I learned. Even for me.

Bruce Manno from the Brewers called to see how I was doing. I said fine and he asked if I intended to be in Arizona for spring training next year.

"I'm not sure, Bruce," I said. "I think it's too early to say. My shoulder feels a lot better, a lot stronger, but I'm not sure I want to go through all that again. You know I'm getting married."

"Yeah, I remember," he said. "Congratulations. Listen, man, I can give you till January first to make a decision. You let me know by then if you're going to come back. If you don't call, I'm going to consider that you don't want to come back. Okay?"

"Okay."

When I said the word I really didn't know which way to lean, other than in the opposite direction of heartache. I would've said yes right then if I'd thought that trying to play again would make me happy. Or would failing again make me fatally unhappy? I'd bought four months to weigh the choice.

Lorri and I planned the wedding to be a lot more modest than the first time. It would be at the Baptist church in Brownwood, with a hundred or so friends and family, and be followed by some coffee and cake and wine in the fellowship hall. But it turned out unimaginably modest when Truman Harlow died two days before the date. He was an old man who'd been a great friend to nearly everyone in Brownwood. People loved him so much that the town's main overpass is named "The Truman Harlow."

Truman was buried at the same time as our wedding. So only a handful of people showed up to throw rice at us. The rest went to the funeral. As they should have.

We stood before God and the minister and vowed to stick together through thick and thin, good and bad, prosperity and poverty. It seemed impossible that our being together would bring more thin than thick, bad than good, poverty than prosperity.

After the ceremony Lorri and I drove the three hours to Austin for a flight to Orange County, California. We checked into the Pacific Princess motel, a pink stucco box across the road from Disneyland and down the way from Knotts Berry Farm, and spent the next four days and three nights in one or the other of the two amusement parks. (Both of us love roller coasters; the bigger the better.) We were husband and wife now, and I could feel that it meant something. The connection between us had been strengthened by saying "I do." We got a kick out of calling each other "husband" and "wife," and our only serious discussion the whole time, over dinner one night, was about children. We didn't want any.

I enrolled in school that fall as a full-time student, taking an ordinary freshman's load. (Lorri was a full-time employee, so I didn't have to pay tuition, saving $350 a unit.) No matter what the field, the class work came easily to me. I didn't understand why I hadn't loved learning before. A life sciences professor suggested that I major in pre-med and become a doctor. The honor society, Gamma Beta Phi, invited me to join. I declared biology as a major.

Life was good. I fit school and studying around my work at the state school and helping Tres with off-season workouts. Lorri traveled around the state giving speeches about Howard Payne. We lived in that little house her mother had bought, made ends meet, and were happy.

The final seconds of December 31, 1987, ticked off without my calling Bruce Manno, and at the stroke of midnight that began January 1, 1988, I ceased being a professional baseball player.

No bells and whistles sounded. The ground remained steady. And no biblical plagues visited my house. The decision to quit was mine alone; I discussed it with no one except maybe Grandpa Ernest's ghost. I was proud, actually, for growing up enough to accept that having the talent and desire for something are no guarantees of getting it. Sometimes you're not supposed to get it, and you never know why. You just have to live with the disappointment and move on.

"Are you sure this is what you want to do?" Lorri asked.

"I don't know if it's what I *want* to do," I said. "It's what I *have* to do. Obviously, I'm not ever going to be healthy enough to pitch major-league baseball. I'll just do something else."

A few days later a letter arrived. It was my release from the Brewers. "Dear James," it began.

The dream was dead. Long live the dream.

CHAPTER SIX

WE CALLED HER BRANDY. No one knew her original name or even her age. She'd just had a litter of pups when someone locked her in the garage and moved away. For two weeks she'd howled and barked and clawed at the aluminum and tried to keep herself and her babies alive. Finally a passerby lifted the garage door. Two of the pups did survive and were adopted out of the shelter right away. But what were the chances that an adult springer spaniel whose spine protruded like an elevated railroad track would find a home before her expiration date in the shelter? She wasn't adorable, like the pups; she looked pathetic.

Lorri and I adopted her and nursed her back to health (and beauty) within a month. Brandy was grateful for every meal and every word and touch of affection. The first time we left her alone she tried to escape by chewing away the windowsills. From then on we took her everywhere with us. She'd earned the right not to be alone. No dog ever behaved better. She'd stay at your feet if you walked with her; when you sat, she curled up under your chair and didn't move; and she'd relax in the car all day without complaint, whether she was waiting or you were driving. We bought a Dodge Caravan minivan for Brandy to roam around in while Lorri took her as a companion (Brandy was a good listener) on her eight- and ten-hour drives to recruit HPU students in far-flung towns. Hotel clerks were only half joking when they said that Brandy was the most agreeable guest they'd ever had. In the high schools where she spoke, Lorri brought Brandy onto the stage and told her to stay, and Brandy wouldn't move until Lorri finished her spiel. Kids told Lorri that Brandy had been the deciding factor in their enrolling at HPU, and later when they were students they visited Lorri's office to see if Brandy was there. Brandy was the child that Lorri and I thought we would never have, and turned out to be one of my best friends.

Too bad I couldn't bring her with me on the long road trips I began making as a driver for the Texas Youth Commission. I traveled all over the state in a twelve-passenger van to pick up juvenile offenders and bring them back to facilities where they were given psychological evaluations and sent to places like the state school in Brownwood. But no dogs were allowed in the van. My companions—and there always had to be two adults—were human. I remember Mrs. Jefferson, a little old lady who liked to linger out on the road as long as possible, collecting overtime. She'd fall asleep in the shotgun seat while I drove; every once in a while she'd wake up and tell me to slow down, then go back to her nap. Some of our trips together lasted fifteen hours. But with Mr. Shipman as my partner, I drove fast. He wanted to get there and back as quickly as I did, and we were once reprimanded for shaving two hours off the normal nine-hour roundtrip runtime from El Paso to Pyote across the most desolate parts of West Texas in 110-degree weather with three young murderers in shackles behind us and no firearms to protect us in case something went wrong. You'd have driven fast, too.

One time we picked up a pretty fourteen-year-old runaway who'd shoplifted whatever she wanted or needed. She had a surly attitude but seemed otherwise harmless, and nobody thought to handcuff her to the van seat, like the six boys. Every time I glanced in the rearview mirror, I saw she'd changed seats. After a while I noticed why. She was, shall we say, manually servicing her fellow delinquents—and wouldn't stop after we warned her. We ended up handcuffing her to the grate separating the drivers from the offenders, then listened to her obscene tirade for the next two hundred miles.

I liked the job but it came with some stress. There was a six-month period when the entire corrections system was on high alert. The authorities had busted a Jamaican drug kingpin outside Houston, and the word went out that Jamaican thugs were coming for revenge and didn't care if they died as long as they took innocents down with them. A man with a Jamaican accent phoned the state school and threatened to break in and kill everyone inside unless we set free a kid they'd used as a courier. He said he knew that we didn't have armed guards. All of us grew eyes in the backs of our heads. A pencil falling to the floor would startle ten people. A car backfiring outside became an assault. The wind against the windows was an invasion. I think I was especially jumpy from lack of sleep; working fifty or so hours a week and going to school and studying and helping Tres with the baseball program didn't leave much time for it. The only place I felt safe and calm was on the baseball field.

When the season began it had been about a year since the shoulder surgery. Tres asked me to work with the pitchers and to throw batting practice to the hitters. I threw without pain. Better, I threw with accuracy; nothing but strikes. I kept thinking, *Where the hell was this when I was playing before?* Better still, from where I stood on the mound, the ball seemed to move faster than before. That didn't make sense. Doctors and pitchers claimed that you lose a couple of miles an hour after every surgery. How could I have gained speed? I estimated ninety miles an hour and figured it was my imagination.

"Hey, you're throwing pretty good," the voice said from behind me. It belonged to Walt Williams. Everyone called him "No Neck" for obvious reasons. He was from Brownwood and had been a big-league outfielder with the Astros, White Sox, Indians, and Yankees from 1964 to 1975. Now he was a minor-league batting instructor for the Texas Rangers and also helped out Tres from time to time. "Maybe you oughta try coming back."

"What did you say?" I asked.

"I said, your arm looks okay. You're throwing like a big leaguer. You want to try? I'll see what I can do."

I was dumbstruck for a second but there was no stopping the giddiness. The only sound from my mouth was laughter, and Walt recognized what it meant.

Dreams die hard. Maybe they never die at all.

By the time I got home that night my fever was high. I told Lorri about Walt and she didn't hesitate. She said, "Why don't you let him make some calls and see if he can get you looked at by scouts?" Having a dog, not kids, gave us that kind of freedom. She wanted her husband to follow his dream and be happy.

All over the country, especially in Texas, there are guys called "roving scouts" who have day jobs outside of baseball but know baseball talent when they see it and can refer the talent to higher authorities. Walt set me up with one—a gynecologist—over in Kerrville. The doctor liked what he saw and called Mark Snipp, a full-time scout for the White Sox in Fort Worth. A week later I drove up there and threw for him. Mark complimented my pitching, made some inquiries, and asked if I could go to Florida instructional ball when it started in the fall.

It was okay with Lorri and okay with my bosses at the state school. They said I'd accumulated so much comp time that I wouldn't even have to take a leave of absence; I could just go and come back. Lorri threw me a surprise party and decorated the house with little white socks.

The time came to pack my bag. "See you in about six weeks," I said to Lorri. I kissed her and rubbed Brandy's belly and flew off to Florida believing that something magical was about to happen, because God really did work in mysterious ways. The last arm surgery had driven me out of playing professional baseball and into teaching it, and in teaching it I had learned more about it than I'd ever known, and now I was capable of understanding that my arm hadn't been the issue, my head had—bad psychology creating bad physiology. What was that quote about people who can't remember the past being condemned to repeat it? That didn't apply to me anymore. Adversity had forced me to grow up, and by growing up I'd finally become worthy of my dream. I was going to be a big-league pitcher. And there were no murderers in my backseat.

Over those six weeks I had a dozen outings of three or four innings each and pitched well in each of them until the last, against the Seibu Lions from Japan. My control was off that afternoon, and they knocked me around, but that didn't dull any of the shine for me or the White Sox. My arm and mind felt strong, and one of the White Sox executives told me that I'd be spending spring training with the triple-A club.

The winter passed quickly. I worked long hours and enjoyed the work knowing that this wouldn't be my career. I took a full load of classes and studied hard not because I needed the degree but because I enjoyed the learning. It was all part of my growing up.

Lorri was busy, too, in the admissions office and on the road. We were like ships passing each other in a safe harbor, a young couple without any real responsibilities to the real world, only to each other.

The night before I left for Florida, a thunderstorm rocked Brownwood. Brandy hated the crack of thunder and as always scrambled under the bed. In the morning she was still there and I had to coax her out. The three of us got into the Toyota for the ride to Abilene airport. I drove. Lorri sat shotgun and kept her hand on my right knee. Brandy knew something was different about this trip. She perched on the backseat and leaned forward, resting her chin on my shoulder and whimpering. I rubbed her head when I stepped out. Lorri and I held each other a long time. Another airport goodbye.

"I'll see you in the big leagues," I said.

"I'll be there," she said as Brandy jumped out of the car onto the curb and nuzzled my leg. "We'll both be there."

The White Sox training camp was in Sarasota, which is on Florida's western coast between Tampa to the north and Fort Myers. The weather started hot, then turned cold, then hot again, as it does sometimes in the late winter there. For two weeks I threw like Cy Young. The White Sox were as excited as I was. Larry Hymes, a team executive, took me aside and said that they intended to start me with the high-A team in Sarasota in order to build up my strength, but that they figured I'd be in the big leagues by the middle of the season. I ran to my hotel and called Lorri to tell her the news. She wasn't home yet from a recruiting trip.

By morning I couldn't get out of bed. You've heard of the swine flu? This was the Texas Chainsaw Massacre flu.

For two weeks I lay in bed, coming in and out of consciousness. I was too sick and too hurt even to fall out of bed, crawl six feet to the window, and glance up at the display of northern lights that for some odd meteorological reason were visible one night; everyone in central Florida saw them but me. I tried to read a book but my eyes couldn't focus, so I kept on CNN as background noise to divert my attention. The big news was the death sentence issued by Iran's religious leader against Salman Rushdie for writing *The Satanic Verses*. Anyone who killed Rushdie, Ayatollah Khomeini proclaimed, would collect a couple of million dollars. In my delirium I considered insulting Mohammed myself, hoping someone would break in and shoot me.

Spring training was almost over when I finally climbed out of bed. The White Sox had me throw on the sidelines for several days, and then camp broke and I left with the high-A team. My first time on the mound came in the sixth inning of a home game in Sarasota. I felt good, and the radar gun said my ball was going ninety. So why were these guys—minor leaguers!—hitting it off the center field wall? I gave myself whiplash from turning to watch the missiles fly overhead.

This wasn't supposed to be happening. This wasn't part of the fantasy. I stood on the mound and felt the ground opening up to swallow me. Something had changed in the world and I didn't know what. Maybe I hadn't figured things out after all. I told myself to forget about today and get back to normal tomorrow.

That night my shoulder started to hurt. But was it pain or just sore? The answer came after my next outing, which didn't go any better than the previous one or hurt any less. No amount of aspirin took the edge off. It was impossible to sleep or even roll over without thinking that a medieval torturer was plying his trade on my shoulder.

I told the White Sox that something had to be seriously wrong and I should have the doctor look at the shoulder. They said I hadn't thrown in a long time and should rest a few days, take some painkillers, and not lose my composure. Composure? I didn't have any composure left to lose. This couldn't be bad psychology creating bad physiology; the flow of creation had been reversed.

I've heard Dr. James Andrews, the orthopedic surgeon in Birmingham, Alabama, referred to as the Dr. Jobe of the South. He was tall and gentlemanly and had the calm, easy manner of someone who does his job as well as it can be done. For a day he ran more tests on me than an SAT examiner. I waited in his office for him and the results.

"Jimmy," he said, "I can't find anything physically wrong with your arm."

At the time I didn't pick up on the word *physically*. By using it he probably meant that my pain was psychosomatic. That fits with what he said next: "We could go into the shoulder and look around, but that would set you back another year or two, and if you really don't want to play anymore, there's no reason to have the surgery at all. You're twenty-five now. What do you want to do?"

"Doctor Andrews," I said, "I think it's time for me to grow up. I need to go back to school and go on with my life. Doesn't look like baseball is it. No matter what I do, I just keep getting hurt. I don't want to be hurt anymore."

"I understand, son," he said.

I sat there as he phoned the White Sox front office and explained that I would be risking permanent damage to my arm if I kept pitching. He listened and nodded and looked at me and hung up. "You're supposed to go back to Sarasota," he said. "They want you to stay awhile and see how you feel."

"Doesn't matter," I said. "Nothing's going to change."

He came around the desk and put his hand on my shoulder, but I didn't feel as bad as you might think. I remembered hearing about a young man who'd had bone cancer in his arm. The pain was excruciating, like liquid fire boiling in his veins twenty-four hours a day. Unable to take it anymore, he chose to have the arm amputated. He woke from the surgery and saw his family gathered around the bed, intending to comfort him. But he felt happy, even after glancing down at the space where his arm would have been lying. Living without pain meant more to him than his arm. That's how I felt. My pain was as much emotional as physical. My childhood dream had become childish. Whatever the reason, I wasn't supposed to pursue it anymore. If I did, I'd only be hurting myself and my wife.

"It's only a game," I said.

I thanked him and opened the door. A patient was standing in the hallway, cooing over the big, newly autographed photo of Jack Nicklaus on the wall.

"Nicklaus was here?" I asked.

"Yeah," he said, "you just missed him."

At the moment I felt worse about that than about my life's next detour. It was a relief to be out of limbo. You can't fight God's will. You have to find what you're supposed to be doing, even if it's not what you want to do.

I made it back to Sarasota and told Larry Hymes that I was retiring. He said the Sox had to pay me my $1,500 monthly salary for the remainder of the season, and I said it seemed like stealing money; I wasn't playing anymore.

He shook my hand and said, "Let me know if something changes, including your mind."

"Sir, nothing's going to change that," I said. "I'm done."

"I've heard that before," he said.

I packed and waited for a flight and thought about this being the first day of the rest of my life, and about letting the future begin today—anything to distract my mind from baseball. You could go crazy trying to understand why guys whose brains were in their shorts and whose gum wrappers were filled with marijuana could have all the fun they wanted and still advance through the ranks.

I stepped off the plane in Dallas. Lorri was waiting in the terminal, uncertain what kind of mood I'd be in. It had been three and a half months, and she looked fantastic. My smile put her at ease. We ate in a restaurant and spent the night in a nearby hotel, and she tiptoed around the subject, letting me know through her affections that she felt sorry for my disappointment but not so sorry that I'd wallow in self-pity; it was a tightrope walk without a net, and she pulled it off.

In the morning we woke in each other's arms and I knew I'd made the right decision. She was my life now.

We were in the car, two hours from home, when she asked, "What're you going to do, Jimmy?"

"Find a job and go to school," I said. That was as specific as we needed to get. She trusted me to do the right thing for both of us.

We pulled into our driveway around noon. Lorri drove off to work. I picked up Brandy from our neighbor's house and spent the rest of the day making up for being gone so long. I promised her I'd never do that again.

The movie *Field of Dreams* opened in town, and I

made the mistake of buying a ticket. It's about a man who hears a voice and builds a baseball field in his Iowa cornfield and does other things without understanding why because his heart has been whispering to his brain that he needs to reconcile with his dead father. When he and his dad finally meet, in a place where the past and the present merge and there's only forgiveness between them, I really did believe for half a moment that such a thing could happen, and tears spilled out of my eyes, and then I felt ashamed for crying—for believing it and for wanting to believe it. But why wouldn't I?

"Is there a heaven?" the son asks.

"Oh, yeah," the father says. "It's the place where dreams come true."

Unfortunately, my life had already been described by another character, an old man who'd had to walk away from baseball fifty years before. He says, "It was like coming this close to your dreams and then having them brush past you, like a stranger in a crowd."

I went home thinking that if heaven's the place where dreams come true, and you only get to brush past your dreams, you must be in hell.

Weeks later I read in the paper that the White Sox had called up rookie pitcher Scott Rudinsky, and I remembered the look on Larry Hymes's face when he'd said he expected me to make the big club that season. He'd seemed sincere, and I'd believed him because I wanted to believe him, and now I knew he hadn't been blowing smoke to soothe me. Scott was behind me on the depth chart.

For people in the real world, authentically historic events happened almost every month in 1989. In March the *Exxon Valdez* spilled millions of gallons of oil into an Alaska sound. In April the Chinese rallied for democracy, and in June they were slaughtered. In November the Berlin Wall fell, the two Germanys were unified, and Czechoslovakia became a democracy. A month later Romania overthrew its Communist dictator and executed him and his wife, and America sent troops into Panama to arrest Manuel Noriega, the country's leader and leading drug dealer.

I was trying to make the real world matter more than memories of what might have been in Jimmy's World, so my retiring from baseball—absolutely, positively, categorically retiring—and deciding never to read box scores again mattered less than all of those events from 1989. But nothing that happened that year, including Tiananmen Square, affected me more than Brandy's dying, in November.

We'd taken her to the vet, and he'd found heartworms. What we didn't know was that those two weeks in the garage without food had damaged Brandy's liver, so that the oral heartworm medication became a kind of poison. The next morning she refused to go to class with me. I left her lying on the blanket we kept for her on the kitchen floor. She looked miserable, and when I came home three hours later she hadn't moved. There was blood pouring from her mouth, and it covered the floor.

I remember gasping and feeling short of breath and beginning to wheeze. I don't remember calling Dad to hurry over with his big pickup truck, but I must've because he showed up and I carried Brandy to the longbed and petted her all the way to the vet's office. When she was put to sleep an hour later, everything got so dark I'd have thought I was dead if it hadn't hurt so much.

Lorri was heartbroken, too. Both of us felt closer to Brandy than to most anyone else, and our tiny house seemed huge and empty without her.

You should know that I know that any connection between Brandy's death and what happened next may exist only in my imagination, but I believe that God writes straight in crooked lines (it's a Portuguese proverb) and that you can only read the lines after they're written and have become the past.

Here's the plot: Lorri applied for a job in the admissions office of Angelo State University, in the city of San Angelo, about three hours southwest of Brownwood, in the heart of dusty West Central Texas. San Angelo was five times bigger than Brownwood, and ASU that much bigger than Howard Payne. The pay wasn't so many times better but the shine on her résumé would be, and anyway Lorri wanted to live in a city that you couldn't drive from one end of to the other in two minutes or less.

"What do you think about moving?" she'd asked before applying. "My job here is a dead end."

"I'll go wherever you want," I'd said. I didn't need to be in Brownwood or at HPU; I was ready for a change, too. "Whatever's best for you."

"You can finish school at ASU."

"I can do it anywhere."

Lorri heard in late December that she'd gotten the job, and in early January we celebrated with a long, romantic weekend in Corpus Christi. I'd never seen her so excited or happy. The only thing I remember talking about is whether I should stay behind in Brownwood and finish up the year at Howard Payne. Lorri said I should stay; if I didn't, I'd lose my credits. "It's only for three months," she said. And we kissed again, thinking about being separated for so long.

We drove down to San Angelo together, looking for an apartment, and found a duplex near the center of things. I liked the city and could see myself living there. There's a city center and upscale homes on one side and shacks across the tracks and a river that flows after heavy rains. There's an amusement park and a livestock auction company and a bordello museum and a perfectly preserved U.S. Army fort from the Indian Wars days, and the first four storefronts in the mall are recruiting offices for the armed services. What I paid most attention to were the parks. Here and there I saw kids playing catch or kicking soccer balls and shooting hoops, and all I could think of was showing up to make friends. How would I do it otherwise? I didn't know how to make friends without sports.

Days before Lorri was supposed to leave, her doctor confirmed what we thought to be true.

She was pregnant.

I counted backward from the due date. It must have happened in Corpus Christi. But how? The odds of a sperm and an egg coming together with a birth control pill as matchmaker are about the same as being struck by lightning. Twice.

Lorri was in San Angelo. I stayed alone in the little house we rented from my mother-in-law. I worked at the school and helped Tres with the baseball team and went to class and studied. At night I'd call Lorri and then hang up and try not to brood. I was twenty-six with a kid due that fall, my wife was three hours away and starting a new job, we were going to have no support from our parents once the baby arrived, my dream had been wiped out, we were broke, and I had to find a new job as soon as I got to a new city where I knew no one. Life was hell. After a few weeks I couldn't stand it anymore and packed up the clothes, bed, and books we'd left behind for me; I notified HPU and the state school and Tres Womack; and a day later I joined Lorri in San Angelo. People told me I was crazy to study that hard for six months and then forfeit the class credits, especially when my grades were going to be A's. But I needed to be with my wife more than I needed fifteen units.

Lorri liked her job but was tormented by morning sickness that lasted into the noon and night. Our duplex was small and cost twice as much as our house in Brownwood, and our new landlord wasn't likely to let us slide for the rent when we were tight, the way my mother-in-law had. We needed money, and the Institute for Cognitive Development Center needed help. It was a sort of halfway house for people whose mental retardation wasn't severe enough to require institutionalization. One man I took care of couldn't feed himself but could assemble a thousand-piece jigsaw puzzle in an hour. I called everyone "sir" and "ma'am" and surprised myself with how much tenderness I felt for these people who had trouble with shoelaces, toilet paper, and door handles; everything was a challenge.

One day Lorri said we needed a new place to live. This one wasn't nice enough for our baby.

That was the moment I caught the maternal light in Lorri's eyes. I rested my hand on her belly and imagined holding "our baby." For the first time I didn't fear what I might do to him. I vowed to remember my childhood and not repeat my parents' mistakes. This child would be welcomed into the world and cherished.

We found a three-bedroom house that cost a lot

more than the duplex. I found a second job as the guy who shows up at the city pool at seven in the morning with the chlorine and chemicals to keep two hundred five-year-olds from turning the 110-degree sun-heated water into a caldron of infectious disease. I vacuumed and sifted the trash, monitored the bacteria levels all day, and kept the pool temperature at a refreshing seventy-eight.

The days rolled by with a kind of numb sameness. Something was missing. Some spark. Enthusiasm. Passion. Not that there was time to feel passionate about much of anything. I came home from the institute and fell into bed and closed my eyes and opened them and went to the pool. In our spare seconds together, Lorri and I talked about the baby or worked on the nursery. She asked me fifty times if something was wrong. "Nothing," I said. She didn't believe me.

One night I pulled up in front of the house and saw her waiting outside. She jumped in the front seat of my car and said, "Let's go."

I didn't have to ask where to. No matter how tired or stressed she is, my wife is always in the mood to do one particular thing. And she can do it for hours without spending a penny.

"Lorri, I don't feel like shopping," I said. "Not tonight."

"Come on," she said. "Just drive. I'll direct you."

I groaned and pulled away and followed her directions. Wherever we were going wasn't near any store I knew. "Where the hell are we?" I said when we passed the U-Catch-Em Catfish Farm. "Come on, Lorri, this is stupid. I'm hot and tired. I want to eat and go to bed."

"Poor baby," she said. "We're almost there. Make a left."

I did and saw it immediately. A ball field. Softball. It was rickety and makeshift—typical West Texas. Dirt surrounded the field and stuck up in places where there should have been grass. A San Angelo water tower stood about a hundred feet beyond the right field fence. It struck me as depressing.

Two teams of guys my age, give or take a half decade or so, were warming up before a game. I hadn't played softball since I was a ninth-grader in Florida. Softball wasn't for men. It was for has-beens and never-wases and wannabes. Softball pitchers threw the ball up in the air and you had to hit it before it dropped on the plate for a strike. It was stupid, and Lorri knew I thought so. So why'd she bring me out here?

"Let's just stop for a minute," she said, getting out of the car.

"You kidding?" I said. "Lorri!"

I sat there and stewed, watching her take a seat in the bleachers behind home plate. It was humiliating. I wanted to drive away. A couple of people turned around to look at me. I pretended to be doing something and then stepped out and climbed up next to Lorri. The players took fielding practice. Then the umpire called "Play ball" and one of the captains came over to the screen and yelled out that he was a man short.

"Anybody wanna play?" he yelled.

I said nothing. Lorri elbowed me. "Come on," she said. "You know you do."

I looked around to see if anyone else planned to take him up on the offer. Lorri pushed me, and I didn't resist. I stood up.

"You?" the manager said.

"I'll play," I said.

"You got a mitt?"

I was about to say no when Lorri said, "Yeah, he does."

I gave her a Jackie Gleason double-take and whispered, "I don't have my mitt."

"It's in your trunk," she said.

I smiled and started to walk to the car, and within a few steps I was running. I put on my mitt, pounded it, and sprinted back to the field. "You're in right field," the captain said, looking at my tennis shoes.

Anybody who's ever played baseball on a playground knows what it means to be in right field. It means you stink. Or the captain thinks you stink. The worst kid on the team, the one who was picked last, gets sent to right. It's where left-handed batters hit the ball, if there are any. And there aren't many. Except on the team we played that night.

The third batter was a leftie who hit a line drive far

down the right field line. It bounced against the wall and would have been an easy double, maybe even a triple, except that I caught up to it on one bounce and whirled and fired a bullet to second base. It sounded like a cap gun when it hit the shortstop's glove, and the batter, trying for a double, was out by ten feet. The crowd oohed.

I ran off the field and into our dugout.

"Hey, what's your name?" the captain said.

I told him and turned around toward Lorri. She waved to me and smiled. This was the first time she'd ever seen me play. Had she engineered this whole thing, or just put my mitt in the trunk out of hope? I didn't need to ask, because even if it was coincidence, I loved her for knowing more about me than I knew about myself. She knew that I'd missed playing, and that I needed the competition and the incredible pleasure of doing that one thing in the world I do incredibly well. Softball or baseball—the rules were the same. Both used bats, gloves, bases, umpires, fences, and foul lines; this was still the game I loved, and I remembered why I'd lain awake and thrown the ball to myself for hours and hit fungo rocks in a field until the dirt ground was bare. I remembered the smell of a leather glove and the sight of a guy sliding into second and the fun of playing again without having to worry about scouts and managers.

Bill, the captain, told me I was batting last. Of

course. The new guy always bats last; he has to prove himself. I watched my teammates swing at the ball. The pitch doesn't come at you fast, like a baseball; it hangs in the air several seconds and falls in your vicinity. Some pitchers loft the pitch so high it brings rain, and the key word is patience. You can't dance the hoochie-coochie while waiting for it.

I didn't get to bat that first inning, and the other team didn't hit anything to right field in the second. I finally came up in the bottom of the second with two outs and two men on, and launched a cannonball against the fence in right-center, about three hundred feet away. It was all I could do not to smile as I stood on second base. Now the chorus of oohs filled the field.

"Hey, man, where you been?" the other shortstop asked me.

That second-inning double was the worst hit I had all game.

By the fifth inning everybody knew my name, and I was trying to remember all the names of guys who'd introduced themselves. Bill asked where I was from. I said I'd just moved to San Angelo because of my wife's job and had just retired from professional baseball.

"Why?" Bill asked.

"My arm," I said.

"Your left arm?"

"Yeah."

"You saying there's something wrong with it?"

"I was a pitcher."

"I believe it."

"It kept getting hurt, and I got tired of it, and it wasn't worth trying anymore."

"Sure doesn't look hurt now."

After the game, Bill and the manager of the team that played before us argued over which team I was going to be on permanently. Neither of them asked whether I wanted to play. They didn't have to.

"I guess it's up to you," the other manager said to me. His name was Jack, and I picked his team, the Athletics. Bill's team only played around San Angelo. The Athletics entered tournaments all over the South, Southeast, and West, and sponsors paid for the travel. We'd be playing the best teams in the country, Jack said. How could I refuse the competition? I thanked Bill and got Lorri, and we walked to the car.

"You have fun?" she asked. She damn well knew the answer.

"It was all right," I tried to say in a deadpan but couldn't finish without laughing.

The next day I bought some softball pants and cleats we couldn't afford.

Most summer mornings in San Angelo break clear and still. By seven, the heat rides in through the open window and sucks the air out of the room. But certain mornings the sky is low and gray. A promise of something wet teases you, a promise you pray will be kept after endless days of sun that wear down your will and make you understand why hell is supposed to be hot.

On this particular morning there was no blue overhead, and a breeze swirled as I bent over the pool to begin vacuuming. I shivered a moment and saw gooseflesh raised on my bare arm. The western sky was red in the rising light, and I remembered the adage "Red sky at morning / Sailor, heed warning." I thought that if the clouds could just hold back the heat, we'd have some weather later, and the thought energized me. My mind wandered and I imagined being a member of the construction crew that had built this pool in the 1930s, under FDR's Works Progress Administration. It wasn't a stretch to compare myself. They were poor guys like me, hungry for work to feed their families. Just the day before, Lorri and I had had to scrape change together for a gallon of milk, and Lorri had dropped it getting out of the car, and it had fallen and broken and Lorri had cried. Our ends didn't always meet before payday, which was today.

By two o'clock the sky was a black gray, and the radios people brought to the pool crackled occasionally with electricity. We couldn't see any of the lightning bolts or hear the thunder, but that static said that it was out there somewhere. In a while the breeze picked up and the temperature fell to the low 90s, and finally you could see the lightning. The thunder still lagged several seconds. Then it didn't. And the rain came. This was a full-fledged thunderstorm, a wild scene of crackling lightning bolts and seismic booms. Kids screamed and scrambled from the pool. The lifeguards closed the facility and sent everyone home for the day. I stayed alone to enjoy the spectacular show, lying in a lounge chair under the awning and sipping a can of Dr Pepper as the storm beat down harder.

The thunder and rain were too loud to hear anything else, so I don't know what drew my attention to the pool entrance behind me, but there stood Lorri. I jumped up and opened the gate and pulled her under the awning. No pregnant woman ever looked more beautiful. Her eyes were bright, her skin taut and clear.

"I was on my way back from a meeting and saw your car," she said. "Isn't this wonderful?"

I held her for a moment and dragged over another chair and bought her a Sprite from the machine. We lay side by side and held hands. Lorri guided my fingertips lightly over her six-month protruding belly. The baby kicked.

"Did I do that?" I asked.

"Well, I guess it knows its daddy," she said.

We stayed that way for an hour, not saying a word—not needing to. Then the rain stopped and swimmers showed up at the pool gate. That broke the spell. Lorri said she had to go. I started to tell her something like "Let's not lose this moment," but the words fell into the mammoth black hole of things I've always wanted to say and haven't. It was hard watching her walk away. I wondered if we'd ever feel just that close again.

If you're new in town, it can take a long time to meet people. Or you can already know a resident who introduces you around. Or you can be a pretty girl and everyone will introduce themselves to you. Or you can be an athlete. It's not as potent as being pretty, but in Texas doors do open sometimes. I needed them to open for me, and they did, when the pool shut down after the summer. Through someone who worked with someone, I lined up a job as an afternoon teacher's aide, helping the Edison Junior High football team that fall and the baseball team come spring. Word had gotten out that I'd played on one of Gordon Wood's championship teams. That bought me more goodwill than pitching a minor-league no-hitter ever would.

It felt right to be on the football field. I liked the kids and had the patience to teach without screaming. That made them like me. Too bad the job was only part-time. Between the school and the institute, I was working twelve hours a day, not sixteen, at minimum wage, and I needed to make up the difference or we'd fall farther in the hole. One evening after practice I stopped at a Town and Country grocery store for a quart of milk and asked the manager if she had any job openings. She talked to me awhile, and I became a cashier five nights a week for five bucks an hour.

Town and Countrys are small, neighborhood markets. San Angelo has about twenty of them, some just a few blocks apart, so customers tend to shop at the same location. You end up learning their names and what they usually shop for, and from that you can guess if they're making it all right or just getting by. Not that it mattered whether someone paid with food stamps or cash. I said "yes, ma'am" and "yes, sir" all the same— until I met Mrs. Hudson, who paid with food stamps and drove away in her new Lincoln Town Car. It made me sick, and after a month I couldn't stand it anymore. I told her, "You should be ashamed of yourself, cheating that way." She lifted her chin like someone who'd had a lot of practice being indignant, and snapped that I was a rude young man, and this was none of my concern as long as the market got its money, and how dare I question her integrity that way, and, well, she'd never set foot in this market again, that's for sure, but would take her business elsewhere, where it was appreciated. I said, "Good!" and she said she'd see to it that I lost my job, and I said I'd rather vacuum outhouses in the dark than be a party to fraud. She sneered and sped away.

My outrage fit her crime, but wasn't really directed at her alone. It was directed at all the Mrs. Hudsons of the world, all those whose blessings would have been better spent on more deserving people. A popular book of the time was *When Bad Things Happen to Good People*, and I remember thinking that there should have been one called "When Good Things Happen to Bad People." I spent forty hours a week changing adult diapers and spoon-feeding poor souls whose only crimes were genetic, and at least an hour watching the news about the half-million American troops massing in the Persian Gulf for a war that Saddam Hussein promised to make "the mother of all wars." During all of those hours, and all the rest, I worried over the birth of my child, who was due any day. How would I take care of him? Would the day care we'd found treat him well? Wasn't it terrible that we both had to work? And what kind of world was this for a child anyway?

Mom and Charles came to help Lorri and me with the birth and baby. On their second afternoon, Lorri took Mom shopping and in the middle of the mall whispered, "Uh-oh, I think I peed on myself."

Mom checked and said, "Your water's broken, honey. Let's get to the hospital."

That was five o'clock. They called me and I rushed there and spent eight hours coaching Lorri to breathe through the labor pains. At two in the morning, we moved into the delivery room. I was standing by Lorri's side, holding her hand, when the doctor said, "Mr. Morris, wouldn't you like to see your son being born?"

To see my son being born. His words gave the moment a new reality. This was actually happening.

I ran over to stand behind him and saw what looked like a head of black hair beginning to emerge. I tottered like a drunk and a nurse righted me in time to see the doctor catch my boy shooting out of the birth canal like a sack of potatoes down a water slide.

Then the doctor said, "Look, you've got a cone-head."

That got my attention in a hurry. "Oh, my God," I said. "What's wrong with my kid?"

His head was squished and came to a point on top. A nurse who didn't think much of the obstetrician's humor quickly explained that this was normal and would correct itself in a few weeks. She began swaddling the baby.

Lorri demanded to hold her son and fell asleep after trying to nurse. The staff took the baby for a bath, and I stepped outside for some air, expecting a temperate breeze. Instead I got a face full of snow. Sometime in the last ten hours the temperature had dropped from eighty to thirty. Swings like that didn't happen in West Texas, at least not in November, and I wondered if it meant something.

We named our boy Hunter (intending to name the next boy, if we had one, Fisher) and brought him home and wouldn't let him out of our sight. Forget the nursery we'd worked so hard to fix up. Hunter slept beside us in a bassinet, and one of us woke every ten minutes to check his breathing.

Within a week I couldn't remember why we hadn't wanted children or what was supposed to be so great about freedom.

There was no way to tell whether the pain in my left shoulder came from lifting adults off the toilet or throwing footballs for my students or holding Hunter. But it was worsening. At times it felt like alcohol on a burn, and I knew I couldn't live with it. Our health insurer sent me to Dr. Ryan, a no-nonsense orthopedic surgeon in San Angelo. I told him my history, and he said he needed to look inside with the arthroscope; if he found something he'd fix it. I scheduled the surgery for the day before Thanksgiving so that I could go back to my jobs the following Monday. When I came to, he showed me the three-inch bone spur he'd pulled from the rotator cuff.

"That's not all," he said. "Your deltoid was so frayed, I had to take out about eighty percent of it."

I asked what that meant.

"Jimmy," he said, "I didn't fix this for you to be able to pitch again. You'll never pitch again. Do you understand? I tightened it as well as I could, but you've got nothing in there anymore. Just bone. Your pitching days are behind you."

"Doctor Ryan," I said, "my pitching days were already behind me. I just don't want to be in pain." It felt better already.

The next morning Lorri and I and Hunter drove to the Baptist encampment outside Brownwood run by Lorri's sister and her husband. It was the place we spent every Thanksgiving, with Lorri's brothers and sisters and their spouses and children, all forty of us staying in the woods by the lake in comfortable cabins used the rest of the year by visiting missionaries. There wasn't a more pastoral setting within a hundred miles. As soon as we finished Thanksgiving supper, I put on my sling and went fishing and thought about my dead-end jobs, and before the weekend ended I'd decided to start Angelo State when the spring semester began.

That decision seemed to fire up my guardian angels. Why else would Coach Morgan at the junior high have offered me a full-time job just at that moment? He asked me to work with the seventh-grade football team at its early morning practices, then help the accredited phys. ed. teachers until noon, and end the day at the high school with the baseball players. I said yes and quit the institute and sent in my Angelo State application.

ASU accepted me and granted my student loan, but the school credited me for only thirty of the sixty-some units I'd completed at Howard Payne. That made me an incoming sophomore instead of junior. Lorri was upset about all the waste. I declared myself a kinesiology major, intending to earn a master's degree, and enrolled in fifteen units of science and general education courses and studied every spare moment. It was sleep and time with Hunter and Lorri that suffered, but I consoled myself with the thought that you sometimes have to do what you don't want to do when you don't want to do it in order to do what you want to do when you want to do it. Or something like that. I figured I was working toward the future and at twenty-seven was still young enough to have a long one.

CHAPTER SEVEN

THAT SPRING, the Angelo State employment board was covered with job listings on three-by-five cards. I read one that suited me and applied and was hired. Then I quit Town and Country and at midnight began as the late-shift security director for the high-rise men's dormitory, sitting until 8:00 A.M. at a desk in the lobby, monitoring the systems and making sure boys didn't sneak in girls. Between crises I studied and watched reruns of *Hogan's Heroes*, and in the morning went straight to Edison, and after lunch from there to Central. Late afternoons I ran home and napped for three hours (if I hadn't already fallen asleep in my planetarium class) before my night classes, and saw Lorri and Hunter only on weekends. We went to church on Sundays. I felt exhausted and lonely, and Lorri slept alone, but we had a little more money, and I was making progress toward a degree.

School ending for the summer would have been a relief, but the dorm closed down and Edison and Central, too, so I was out of work until the pool hired me back to be the maintenance man. I had time on my hands. I played with Hunter and helped my mother-in-law move to San Angelo. It was a comfort to know she'd be there for her grandson.

One day I drove by the Angelo State football practice field, where the punter was practicing by himself. I stopped to watch through the fence and remembered seeing him punt at the homecoming game a week before Hunter was born. He'd averaged maybe thirty-seven yards a kick, and I'd whispered to Lorri that I could've run out on the field right then, after not punting for nine years, and done better. She'd called me a snob. Now there he was again, still averaging about thirty-seven, even without big linemen and powerful backs rushing him. I drove away and started thinking and made some inquiries. A few afternoons later I came back to the field with my own football and booted a few that went over fifty yards, then walked into the coach's office and said, "I want to punt for you."

The ASU Rams' coach was Jerry Vandergriff, a short, graying man with a face lined by years in the sun. He'd coached at Angelo State, a Division II school, for over twenty years and seemed content. This was home to him.

He looked me up and down and suppressed a giggle. "You do, huh?" he said. "Who are you?"

"I'm Jim Morris. Lorri Morris's husband." Everybody knew Lorri by then.

"How old are you?"

"Twenty-seven. And I have three years of NCAA football eligibility left. I checked."

"Uh-huh." He was humoring me now. "And what experience do you have?"

"Well," I said, "I was an all-state punter and kicker for Gordon Wood."

"Really? How long ago?"

"Not long enough ago to make me worse than the guy you've got now."

I think if I'd dropped anyone else's name but Gordon Wood's I'd have been shown the door. But the thought intrigued him. He knew his punter's limitations and that his football team needed improving, and he knew as well as I did that one of the fastest ways to improve a team is at the punt position. A good punter can bail out an inept offense and give the defense a head start by pinning back the other team closer to its own goal.

"Tell you what," Jerry said, handing me a bag of

footballs, "you take these and get your stroke down and I'll see you when practice starts in August. We'll see what you got."

For the next month and a half I heard a lot of snickering about wanting to play football. "At your age?!" Ha ha ha ha ha. The gibes didn't come from Lorri, who knew I could play well but was concerned that football would affect my schoolwork or income (I promised it wouldn't); they came from almost everyone who hadn't seen me punt yet. The funny thing was how their reaction affected me. In the old days I might have felt foolish and embarrassed and changed my mind. The new me wanted it that much more and needed to prove them wrong.

Maybe that came from being married to Lorri. She's one person you don't say "can't" to; she'll do something out of spite, even if it kills her. I remember a softball tournament in Steamboat Springs, Colorado, when she was six months pregnant. We'd gone hiking with my teammates and their wives and girlfriends, and had started up a treacherous, granite trail alongside a waterfall when our well-meaning catcher suggested that, in her "condition," she should wait for us below.

"Oh, yeah? Well maybe *you* should wait below," she'd said, and kept up step for step. Not till the descent, fighting gravity's pull on her big belly, had she encountered problems. "I didn't think of that," she'd whispered to me.

On the first day of football workouts, I walked onto the field wearing a T-shirt and shorts and saw all the other players dressed in practice uniforms with full pads and helmets. I was carrying the bag of balls Coach Vandergriff had given me.

"I'm ready to punt for you," I said.

Players snickered. One of them yelled out "Gramps" and bent over laughing.

"Well, we'll see what you got," Vandergriff said. "Hang around."

I paced the sidelines to warm up while Jason, the other punter, stretched his hamstrings and calf muscles and Achilles tendons. I didn't stretch because I was too tight to stretch, but he couldn't have known that and may have suspected I knew some new technique he didn't. You could see he was nervous. He thought his scholarship was at stake.

The time came. Jason used the classic form he'd learned as a teenager in summer kicking camps that had cost his parents thousands of dollars—more, probably, than his scholarship was worth. The ball came off his foot and arced in a high spiral that traveled thirty-seven yards with three seconds of hang time. A good punt returner would have brought it back for a touchdown.

My first punt, in terrible, clumsy form, sailed sixty yards with five seconds of hang time.

That stopped the snickers and began the coaches talking among themselves. One of them yelled for me to kick it out of bounds as close to the goal line as possible. I put it out on the three-yard line.

"Hey, Morris," Vandergriff shouted. "Go on in and pick up a uniform."

You could see Jason deflate. I walked over to tell him not to worry about losing his scholarship. NCAA scholarship rules prohibited you from making more than a certain amount, even if you made it by sweeping hospice floors. I said I earned above the limit and that my family needed every penny of that and more, so there was no danger of my taking his place on anything other than the field. That didn't ease the hurt of getting beaten out by a decrepit specimen like me, but it softened his attitude.

The clubhouse attendant handed me a set of pads, a jersey, and some pants, and assigned me a locker. It was the one on which a hand-written sign hung: "Old Man." The next day when I came in there was a bottle of Geritol inside it. By then everyone called me "Gramps."

Four of us auditioned for the role of kicker—the guy who kicks off at the beginning of the game or after halftime and following touchdowns. One of the four was the field goal kicker and one was Jason. The first guy, a third-string tackle, teed up the ball and sent it down to the twenty; not very good. The field goal kicker (his was a job I didn't covet) put it to only the twenty-five. Then Jason took a long run-up and smashed a high, end-over-end kick to the five-yard line. The team cheered. You could hear them buzzing, "He's definitely got it."

My turn came last. I teed up the ball, stepped back five yards, and swung my leg as hard as I could. The ball sailed past the end zone and kept going over the goalposts and out into the street—an easy eighty yards. People called me Hercules, and a little later Freddie Jonas, the quarterback coach, pulled me aside and said he'd been watching me throw the ball on the sidelines and run sprints to get warm, and he asked quietly about my maybe quarterbacking the team. I laughed and said my schedule was too full to take on that responsibility. Punters didn't have to practice three hours a day, like the rest of the team. I needed that time to work and study and, if there was any time left, to see my family. Thanks but no thanks. It was crazy enough, I said, to be doing this at twenty-seven.

"Crazy like a fox," he said.

"Crazy like an idiot," I said.

"If you punt like you can, the NFL's gonna come knocking."

"Not on my door, it isn't. I'm too old, Coach. You know that."

"Then why're you doing this?"

"I miss the competition."

I did. Softball was fun, and I'd become the best player around San Angelo, playing about 130 games a year and hitting home runs and winning home-run-hitting contests for cases of Miller Lite and traveling to Mexico and Louisiana and Florida for four-day tournaments on a team that placed second nationally. But something was missing inside. I felt a familiar emptiness that I hoped football would fill.

School started and practices started and my jobs started, and suddenly I began remembering the previous year as the golden age of leisure. I was exhausted twenty-four hours a day.

Then came the first game of the season. Our captain called heads and it came up tails. That meant I had to kick off first. If I'd been any more nervous I would've been hospitalized and under sedation. It felt like seasickness. My hand shook so violently I needed help setting the ball on the tee. Some of that must have been adrenaline, the kind that allows mothers to pick up the back end of Chevys when their children are hurt, because when the referee blew the whistle I booted the ball so hard it hit the goalpost's left upright and bounced back to the thirty-yard line. Someone estimated it would've gone a hundred yards. My punts were struck with the same kind of savagery.

The team's bus rides reminded me of the minor leagues. We crowded into what they now called "motor coaches," but they stank anyway, for trips across Texas and into Oklahoma and New Mexico that sometimes lasted thirteen hours. I used the time going there to catch up on sleep, and the time returning to study. Every school we played was in the middle of nowhere, like San Angelo. Wind was often the game's biggest factor. With thirty-mile-an-hour gusts at its back every other quarter, our offense rolled up the score and didn't need to punt. But the next quarter, when the teams changed direction and the wind was in its face, our offense punted every fourth down (while the other offense ran up the score). That meant I generally punted into the wind—and still averaged over forty yards a punt. I can remember only one of my punts being returned, in the game against Eastern New Mexico. It was memorable because I ran to tackle the ball carrier and got clipped by a blocker and smashed my helmet on the turf and suffered a concussion. The doctor forced me to sit out the next game, against Abilene Christian. That Saturday turned out to be the first day in years that the winds stilled across West Texas. Watching Jason punt thirty-eight yards, I figured I'd have averaged seventy. Our team finished the season with a record of seven and three.

Lorri and I talked about my not playing the following year. "You're going to be twenty-eight," she reminded me. "Your friends are all eighteen and nineteen."

That was true. My best friend was John Mark, a freshman tight end. We'd met when he pitched and played first base for Central High. Now we were on the same team and the ten-year difference between us didn't matter to me or to him. Maybe it was that athletes are naturally immature; playing games is what joins them together. Or maybe my childhood had crippled my expectations of best friendships; no emotional intimacy was required or expected. It didn't matter that I was a married man and a father, hanging out with kids too young even to drink legally. We didn't discuss the state of American ethics or world politics or the psychological benefits of breast-feeding. I couldn't imagine double-dating with them and their girlfriends; the gulf between them and my wife was too wide. And I think that's what hurt Lorri most of all. I can't blame her. My life as a football player excluded her.

"I like being around the guys," I said. "I like playing."

"At least your softball teammates have families," she said.

I said I was earning as much as possible and taking as many units as possible and getting A's in class. It did burn me, though, that her paycheck was larger than all of mine put together, but what could I do? As long as I

worked toward the degree, that would change someday, and not playing football wasn't going to change
anything other than my mood. My mother called Lorri
and said, "When is that boy going to grow up?"

Lorri was a little less delicate. "Just promise me,"
she said, "that you'll be through with school and done
with athletics before Hunter gets to college. I don't
want you two competing against each other." I couldn't
tell whether she was kidding.

My teammates voted me captain. The team, especially the offense, wasn't as good, so I had a lot more
opportunities to punt with the wind at my back. Entering the last game, against Texas A&I, I needed to average forty-three yards or better on eight punts in order
to lead the nation. Before the game I was practicing on
the fifty-yard line. I heard footsteps behind me, heavy
breathing, and a booming voice: "I'm gonna knock you
on your ass today, old man." I whirled around and
stared straight into the chest of a helmeted giant wearing shoulder pads. "You're mine," he said ominously.

"You should respect your elders," I said—after he
walked away.

My first punt was from the back of the end zone
into the teeth of a wind, and I sent it to the other team's
thirty-five. Twelve punts later, averaging forty-nine
yards (only because I took my eyes off the last punt and
shanked it), I won the NCAA Division II punting
championship and made consensus All-American. But

no NFL teams called or sent scouts. Just as I'd predicted.

"Maybe next year," Coach Jonas said.

The following January I turned twenty-nine. I was getting old, and it was getting hard to justify doing anything that didn't further my family's prospects. So when the men's dorm director moved to Dallas in March, I applied for his job. The hours would be long, but the $1,300 salary was more than I had been making. We'd also be able to move into a family suite and pay no rent and eat free meals. I said we might finally buy some breathing room. The catch was that the job ate much of the day and night, and I'd have time for only six scholastic units. That meant two things. The first was that earning my degree would take a lot longer. The second was that I'd have to give up football: You needed twelve units a semester to qualify as a full-time student—and only full-time students could play.

Both of those were good reasons not to take the job. But neither mattered enough to dissuade me. The job was offered and I took it without looking back. I even quit half my classes before the semester ended.

What a strange thing it was to suddenly supervise ten resident assistants, secretaries, a maintenance staff, security directors, and five hundred student residents. Nothing in my background had prepared me for being boss. By temperament, I shared more in common with Cap'n Crunch than Captain Kirk, and yet the job called for real leadership. Besides all the administration, there was a lot of organizing to be done—sports competitions between floors, homecoming floats, blood drives, community awareness presentations, socials with the women's dorm. And then there was discipline. I had to enforce the rules and become surrogate father to hundreds of teenagers. I showed I was a good listener and said my door was always open.

Of course, that wasn't compatible with marital happiness. Lorri and Hunter and I shared a two-bedroom suite on the first floor. It was small and cramped but free. Lorri spent as little time in it as possible, coming home late and leaving early. Her friends weren't college students anymore; mine were. Yes, she was grateful for the uptick in our finances and the freedom it gave us, but at the same time that freedom looked a lot like a jail cell. For Lorri, the dorm was just a mirage in a desert of debt. The longer we stayed there, the longer it would take me to earn my degree and the longer we'd be in adolescent limbo.

She accused me of being a "professional student" and counted up all the student loans I owed. It aggravated her that I'd enrolled in classes and dropped them but still had to pay back the money.

"Just get your degree," she said. "Get it in something. It doesn't matter what. A lot of employers, all they want to know is that you've got that degree. That way they know you have the dedication to stick it out."

I said, "I'm doing the best I can."

"I can see you working with kids. I can see you coaching. If you can't play yourself, you can help them play. At least give yourself that chance. Finish school. Just finish."

I said, "I'm doing the best I can."

The truth I couldn't acknowledge at the time was that we were still paying the price for all those years I'd followed my dream. It just didn't seem fair that the punishment lasted so long. Would it ever end?

At least Hunter seemed happy. He was two now, going on twelve, and had five hundred playmates. The dorm to him was like a sleepaway camp for the highly gifted and talented, because his playmates were college students, not toddlers. They didn't crawl around the floor with him and bang trucks. They talked to him. They played word games with him. And that adult contact fed his precocity. It sometimes scared me, how smart Hunter was. The boy had learned to talk—in full sentences—before he walked. He loved words. Even without understanding what they meant, he ran around saying "kinesiology" and "Copenhagen." Their sounds intrigued him. He watched the Weather Channel for hours, waiting for information on tornadoes and hurricanes, and pretended to be a weatherman reporting on imaginary meteorological conditions that he'd drawn on paper. We bought him a home planetarium so that he could lie in bed at night and study the heavens. There was no keeping up with the rate at which he devoured new information. It was a good thing my mother-in-law lived in San Angelo. She'd been a teacher and knew how to feed his hunger for learning.

I spent most of my time outside the dorm with John Mark and Rob McClellan, who was one of my resident assistants in the dorm. Both of them were big and strong and athletic, and our friendship was about athletics and loyalty and school. We were best friends the way junior high school boys are best friends.

Out of nowhere, Lorri suggested that we have another baby. If we didn't, she said, Hunter would be an only child, and only children are supposed to be lonely children. I couldn't argue. Besides, it made sense that God wouldn't have made sex so much fun unless he wanted us to have siblings. What better way to prepare for the agony and ecstasy of adulthood than to grow up with a brother or sister you can't stand but love to death? It's divine genius.

The question of whether Lorri could or should get pregnant was still unanswered. Three of her sisters had developed a rare kind of cancer after their first births that prevented them from further pregnancies, and there was a possibility that Lorri might have the same condition but undiagnosed.

I think she became pregnant the first night we tried. Even before she missed a period, morning sickness set in. It was the kind of nausea that chemotherapy patients describe. The sight and smell of food twisted her stomach. I remember cooking dinner for Hunter and me in our little kitchenette some nights and Lorri coming home from work. She'd run into the bedroom and slam the door behind her until I cleared the air of any whiff. She was miserable, but found solace in an old wives' tale passed on by a colleague who claimed that the sicker you are, the healthier your child is.

"This baby must be real healthy," she moaned.

One afternoon my secretary handed me the phone and said it was Lorri.

"I have to get to the hospital," Lorri said, her voice full of panic. She'd left work and was calling from our apartment.

I ran down the hall. She was sitting in a pool of blood, crying. I tried to calm her with soothing words, but inside I felt sick and scared. Was this the cancer?

"I lost the baby," Lorri whispered between sobs.

The hospital staff strapped an ultrasound monitor to her abdomen, and the doctor pointed to the baby's beating heart on the screen.

"Your baby's fine," he said. "And there's no indication of a tumor or any form of cancer. Everything's A-OK."

What about the blood?

"It's possible," he said, "that you were pregnant with twins and lost one. That's just a guess. We sure don't want to go poking around in there now. Anyway, you're fine and your baby's fine. I just want you to stay in bed, flat on your back, for two weeks. After that you can go back to normal, except don't work out more strenuously than walking."

Lorri and I held each other. It's funny how a near-brush with tragedy makes ordinary life seem blissful. And it's sad how quickly bliss passes.

After she was back on her feet, Lorri announced she wanted to move out of the dorm. "I can't live here with two kids," she said.

"All right," I said, "but with the money we'll have to spend on rent, it's going to be like taking a seven- or eight-hundred-dollar pay cut."

"I know, Jimmy. But you understand. I know you do."

"Yeah, I do." And I did.

We found a three-bedroom house on Colorado Street, near the university, for six hundred dollars a month, and I began looking for another job, because the only good reason for me to remain dorm director no longer existed. The newspaper said that the city of San Angelo needed a recreation coordinator. Of the sixty-four applicants, I was among the few who didn't have a college degree or better. But Don Hill, the assistant city superintendent, knew me from softball and city basketball leagues and also the pool. He recognized that being coordinator played to my strengths. I planned and set up programs for young people; organized adult athletic leagues; devised senior citizen demonstrations; bought equipment; hired karate and dance instructors; made sure that the city basketball, baseball, and football camps ran smoothly; edited a city recreation magazine; and administered arts and crafts festivals.

I needed only twenty units to earn my degree, and Don said he didn't mind if I finished work at nine in the morning as long as I put in at least forty hours and did the job—and he could reach me when he needed to.

"Go ahead and take the classes," he said, issuing me a pager. "You just be here when you hear the beeps."

Even with the pager it was clear that I couldn't handle more than six units a semester. The classes remaining to earn my degree in kinesiology weren't walkovers; they were subjects like biomechanics. But where things really got hard was in my other major, psychology, which I'd declared the year before—not out of a desire to work in a clinic but out of a need to understand me and what made me tick. I knew I had problems. I was a perfectionist, never satisfied with anything, happy only for moments at a time, never completing anything to my satisfaction. I thought that by studying the mind I might undo my childhood lessons and start life as an adult. It seemed to me that the cause of all my problems was that loud voice in my mind, that one that echoed my father, the one that screamed, "Children should be seen and not heard." I was of adult age and size and responsibilities, but inside I still felt like a child, one who couldn't communicate pain and hurt or even happiness to his wife. In the past, I'd been beat for speaking my mind, so expressing myself now was as hard as trying to climb out of a mud pit in the rain. The list of what I needed to tell my wife but couldn't was a history of our problems. It destroyed me that she was our major breadwinner and that I'd been treading water in nowhere jobs. The memory of my broken dreams ached like arthritis. And there was no way to explain why my smiling more when I played softball than I did when I spent time with her wasn't a reflection on our relationship. She'd cry, "You're happier on that field than you are with me."

It couldn't have been a coincidence that one of the few classes I had left to complete was abnormal psych. On my way back to work from enrolling in that class, I passed a motel with a message board out front that said, "You cannot become what you need to be by remaining what you are." I thought about that for a long time. What was it that I needed to be? And what was I remaining?

My daughter Jessica was born in October. You could see from that first day she was a ham and a flirt. She didn't need to talk, like Hunter. She communicated and got what she wanted with a mischievous smile and a bat of her long black eyelashes. Lorri called her "Miss Thing" (pronounced *thang*), and I told her I was happy with my two children but that I'd love to have a third if it was guaranteed to be another girl.

I remember driving one night to softball in John Mark's new Jeep Wrangler with the open top, telling him how Hunter was my buddy and Jessica was Daddy's little girl and you'd have to be a father yourself to understand the difference. He nodded his head, and suddenly I saw a gap between us and stopped talking in midsentence and grabbed the roll bar above me, as though to steady myself; it seemed John Mark was driving too fast and I was too old. This was what Lorri meant, and I wondered if it signaled the beginning of the end.

Then John Mark said, "Hey, why'd you stop? I love hearing that stuff. I want to know all about being a father. I can't wait."

"Maybe you can baby-sit," I said, "and see what it's like." I was kidding him, but he took me seriously.

"That's a deal," he said, reaching between the bucket seats for a cassette to put in the stereo. He couldn't find the right one and looked down to search for it among the dozen or so.

His eyes were off the road. I said, "Let me get it," and he said, "No, I've got it," and I screamed his name because he'd drifted into the oncoming traffic. He yanked the wheel back and the Jeep went out of control and rode up on two wheels. When we were safe again, he laughed and said, "You're white as a ghost."

"You almost killed us," I said. "What's that show on MTV? *Dead at 21*. That's going to be you, man."

I cinched my seat belt tighter and noticed John Mark wasn't wearing his. I considered ragging on him for it, but I wasn't his wife or father; I was his friend, and friends didn't rag on friends. He pulled into the parking lot and oversteered the wheel back and forth when he saw Rob, turning the Jeep into Mr. Toad's Wild Ride. We laughed and then played ball, and I hit a monster home run to beat their team.

It was the July Fourth weekend of 1995. My softball team drove to Albuquerque for an important regional tournament. Lorri's mom stayed with the kids, allowing Lorri to come along. I always had more fun at these things when she did. She liked them, too, because the other wives were about her age and had children about the same age. These softball tournaments were the only times we spent together without the kids. They were short, paid vacations that gave us a chance to find each other again. Too bad there weren't any two-week tournaments.

I was in the shower after a game when one of my teammates came to our room and said he needed to tell me bad news: John Mark and Rob had been on their way to a softball tournament their team had entered in

Sanderson, Rob's hometown a couple hundred miles southwest of San Angelo, when John Mark's Jeep overturned.

"How bad?" I asked.

He put his hand on my shoulder. "Rob's dead," he said. "And John Mark's barely hanging on." He explained that no other cars were involved, and I figured that John Mark had rolled the Jeep while looking for a tape.

I got dressed in a kind of haze while Lorri packed for us. We drove all night back to San Angelo. I wished I could've cried.

When we walked into John Mark's hospital room, his father hugged me and said, "I'm glad you're here, Jimmy. We waited for you."

John Mark was on life support, with no chance of recovery. They'd been keeping him alive these two days until I came to say my goodbye.

I looked down at his bruised and bandaged face and head, and all the tubes sticking out of him, and there was no way to say a proper goodbye. How do you say goodbye to the best friend you've ever had, a twenty-two-year-old with dreams of being a helicopter pilot, knowing that the only helicopter he'd ever ridden in was the one that airlifted him to the hospital?

John Mark's father nodded to the doctor. In moments John Mark's heart registered as a flat line on a monitor.

Rob's funeral was held the next day in Sanderson.

Mike Robison, my softball teammate, insisted on driving me in his truck—to keep an eye on me for the twelve hours there and back. Mike is a big, powerful guy with a personality to match. He understood that the deaths had created a vacuum in my heart, and he knew I'd fill that vacuum with nothing useful. He was right. I stewed most of the way to Sanderson, angry at Lorri for not taking off of work to join me.

There was only one route from San Angelo to Sanderson. We saw several cars stopped at a point that Mike said had to be the accident site. He pulled over. A young woman stood on the shoulder, staring down at some cassettes, clothes, a shoe—debris from John Mark's Jeep that had fallen out of the open top.

"Are you Jimmy Morris?" she asked. "I'm John Mark's sister, and I just want you to know how much my brother loved you." She put her arms around my neck and held me for a long time. "You meant so much to him."

Things went pretty much to hell in a hurry. These were not my finest hours. I couldn't control my grief or share it with my wife. The place I felt safest and spent most of my time was on the two-thousand-acre ranch for which Mike was caretaker. It was in the middle of nowhere, and I could sulk or shout without anyone asking me to explain myself; that would have been impossible anyway. Mike and I hunted and fished and drank beer, and I went home late every night and pretended to be normal. Lorri saw my absences as a betrayal. But I wasn't much more than an emotional retard and couldn't see past my own pain to anyone else's—not my wife's, not my children's. It was pure narcissism. I'd learned in a psychology class what it looked like, but knowing about it and acting on it were as different as hearing Latin and speaking Latin. My pain was an untreated cancerous tumor. The more I hurt, the more license I granted myself to act out. At some point, even I realized that it had long ago stopped being about John Mark and Rob; what it *was* about, I didn't know.

In all this insanity I managed to keep my job and go to classes and study and earn A's, and in August of 1996, after one last summer psychology class, I graduated Angelo State with a bachelor's degree.

This was the day thousands of days in the making, and it should have been a celebration. I was thirty-two years old and had started college fourteen years before. My being a professional student had built a rickety bridge between my wife and me. Lorri's being the major breadwinner had tormented me and kept me distant. And now the graduation was giving us a chance to begin again. But there was no real joy. I didn't feel particularly proud of myself or relieved or anxious to make up for lost time.

Lorri and the kids, Mom and Charles, Dad and his wife Teresa, and my two grandmothers attended the ceremony in the stadium. When the dean handed me my diploma and wished me well, I fantasized that he was a manager, handing me the baseball with an order to throw strikes. The diploma seemed like a booby prize.

Lorri heard about an opening for an assistant baseball coach at Abilene Christian University. Abilene was nearly three hours north of San Angelo, and when I made the interview appointment, I didn't think about having to commute; I just needed the job and figured the rest would take care of itself. As soon as I walked in, the athletic director apologized and said that they'd just that hour hired a high school coach from Haskell. That meant there had to be an opening at Haskell High, even if its athletic director didn't yet know about it. I drove straight to Haskell, another hour north, and applied for the two-hour-old vacancy. The principal, Greg Melton, stared at me as if I were a godsend. He was a little older than I, but with his perfectly groomed blond hair and unlined face, and wearing a blue suit, he looked younger. We talked awhile and he studied my résumé and said that he'd have to take it up with the school board but that he believed I'd have the job by the next day. This being mid-August, with school about to start, it would have been stupid to turn away a good applicant. Besides, he liked me.

The next afternoon he called and offered me the job. It paid $24,000. I hadn't made that much since my baseball signing bonus, thirteen years before. But I would be earning every penny of it as an assistant football coach, girls' junior varsity basketball coach, girls' assistant varsity basketball coach, boys' head baseball coach, and a biology teacher, leading three classes a day. The teaching required an emergency certificate that the school board granted because of my science degree. State law said I could teach three years with it but would then have to earn the real thing.

Commuting from San Angelo would be impossible. Lorri offered to quit her job at Angelo State, move with me to Haskell, find a new job in Abilene, either at Abilene Christian or one of the other universities there, and commute an hour each way. I said no.

"What do you mean, no?" she asked. "Are you saying what I think you're saying?"

"I'm not happy," I said.

"I'm not making you happy?"

"Nothing's making me happy."

"Look, Jimmy," she said, "I know I'm not the easiest person to live with, but I never want to stop trying. I told you before we got married that when I say 'I do,' it's forever. We've been together over ten years and have two children. That means something. You don't just walk away from that."

"Lorri, I love you, but I'm not in love with you. I can't be, because I don't love myself." I'd read that in a psych textbook or heard a professor say it. I didn't even understand what it meant.

The conversation continued and I said some nasty

things I'll regret until I die, and then I packed a bag and drove away and tried to think about nothing instead of the fact that I'd left my wife.

I found a little furnished apartment in Haskell and worked fourteen hours a day. I was either on the field with one of my teams or teaching my biology classes to ninth- and tenth-graders. The surprise was how easily the teaching came to me and how much at home I felt in the classroom. My students seemed to master the material and enjoyed the work. Mr. Melton told me after a few weeks that he'd been hearing from the kids how well I was doing and how much they liked me, and he asked whether I'd consider signing on for another year. I said yes.

So why couldn't I be happy? All these years I'd blamed our marital problems on money. If only we had more of it, then I'd be happy. If only I didn't have to work three jobs and go to school, then I'd be happy. If only I could sleep more than three hours a night, then I'd be happy. Now, I had one job and eight hours of sleep, and between Lorri and me we were pulling down sixty grand a year—more than enough to pay our bills and live well in West Texas, as long as we did it together. And I couldn't move past myself. The word *sabotage* comes to mind. I drank more than usual and dated a few times. Nothing helped. On Friday nights I met Lorri halfway on the road between Haskell and San Angelo to pick up the kids for the weekend, and on

Sunday nights passed them back, like batons. Coming or going, I barely looked Lorri in the eye. I could see, though, how thin she'd gotten; not the healthy kind of thin. My kids looked at me as if I was rent-a-daddy. Hunter was going on five, Jessica was two, and the distance between us had become a canyon. Hunter told me Lorri cried a lot and that she wouldn't really explain why. He said she said to ask Daddy. "Sometimes things don't work out the way you plan," I tried to explain. But Hunter was too smart. He knew who deserved the blame.

To an outsider, Haskell seems like any little town in Texas. It's in an area called the "Rolling Plains," known for wheat, cattle, and cotton. Compared to San Angelo, there was nothing to do in Haskell. It was a Church of Christ town, and the Church's strict adherence to Scriptures gave the town its personality. No dancing, no drinking, no musical instruments in church; the choir sang a cappella. You either knew people or you didn't, and unless you belonged to a congregation, you didn't meet many because they believed everyone who didn't belong to the Church of Christ was holding a one-way ticket to hell. I had to admit that mine was a miserable little existence, and I never shook the guilt of what had caused it.

Something changed me a week before Thanksgiving, when Lorri and I handed off the kids. I looked at her face—and it somehow looked different. *Peaceful* is the best word. My impression was that she'd made her peace and moved on; she'd faced the worst and cried a bucket of tears and survived the stronger for it.

I said nothing, of course, but the image registered and wouldn't fade. It started me thinking that maybe I hadn't fallen out of love with Lorri—the real Lorri, the Lorri I'd once fallen in love with. Maybe the years and struggle had crushed her spirit, the way it had crushed mine. Or maybe it hadn't crushed mine at all, only hers, so that she'd stopped being Lorri until I got out of her way long enough for her to become herself again. And now that she had, I could see her clearly again and remember why I'd wanted to spend my life with her once upon a time. It's also possible, just possible, that her independence scared me.

For Thanksgiving supper, I drove to Mom and Charles's house in Abilene. His three children and their spouses and children were there. Mom said I seemed unusually quiet, and everyone laughed because only the dead could be quieter. But Mom was right. I couldn't take my mind off Lorri and the kids. They were at the Baptist encampment in Brownwood, with her family. This was the first year I hadn't been in about a dozen.

That weekend lasted forever, and on Monday I called her to talk. She seemed surprised. I asked her on a date and held my breath before she said yes. We met at a midway café and drank tea. We actually laughed. A few days later we did the same. It felt like our honeymoon. Lorri mentioned that she'd involved herself with our church and joined a support group and gotten the kids involved, too. I found myself listening as much to how she talked as to what she said. I found myself appreciating her. She was beautiful again. I remembered believing that Lorri was a woman of substance, a woman to grow old with, a woman capable of making me a better person.

I said, "Maybe we should try to get back together."

She didn't jump at the opportunity, and I was glad. It confirmed my good feelings.

"You know, Jimmy, I'm not a light switch," she said. "You don't just switch me on and everything's going to be okay again."

"I know that," I said.

She said, "There was some reason you felt the way you did, and we weren't communicating about it. So even if we do try to get back together, we have to change the way we do things, or it's gonna turn out the same way again."

"I know," I said.

"But do you know what it means?"

"Yeah, I'm going to have to start talking."

My face must've done something revealing, because she laughed. But I really did want to talk to her, or at least to try. And that felt different.

It was the ghost of Ernest that made me stay at

Haskell until the end of the school year, instead of going home with Lorri that night. His voice said that to walk out now on the school and the kids would have been wrong, and he was right, but where had that voice been when I left Lorri and my own kids?

I had to ask Mr. Melton to let me out of my contract for next year, which I'd already signed. I said, "I appreciate your giving me this big opportunity to work here, sir, but my family has to be more important to me now. I'm sorry, but I think I need to move home and work on my marriage."

Legally, he didn't have to say yes. He could have forced me to stay. But he said, "Jimmy, I have all the respect for your decision," and wished me the best and offered his help in the future any way I wanted it.

I moved back to San Angelo, and we were back to poverty, living on just Lorri's paycheck. It would have been a waste of time to apply for a coaching job at a local school. Even without a Starbuck's, this was a prime Texas town; attracting good teaching help was easy. Finding a job for me within commuting distance might be impossible. But at least Lorri and I were back together. If I had to be a janitor, it was worth it.

CHAPTER EIGHT

AS I RECALL, 1997 was the year the Internet came alive in Texas. Or maybe that was just my perspective, because that was the year it came alive for me. Lorri checked an Internet coaching site for the state of Texas on her work computer and printed out the listings, then brought them home and we pored over them together. I'd make inquiries and hear that the jobs were already taken. It was August now, just before the start of school, and we were desperate. I called Mr. Melton in Haskell, thinking I might be able to walk into my old position, but the vacancy had been filled. We were in a do-or-die situation, and I began looking in the classifieds for any job. Then Lorri came home with a listing for an assistant football and head baseball coach at Reagan County High School in a little town named Big Lake, seventy miles west of San Angelo.

There's nothing memorable about the barren highway between San Angelo and Big Lake, unless you're impressed by having to dodge deer in the road or passing the carcasses of those that weren't dodged. The burnt, flat landscape reminds you of the Sonora desert, the scenery decorated only by power poles and telephone lines. But as I pulled into town I remembered passing through Big Lake years before and wondering how anyone could live in such a place—or why he'd want to. It's the stereotypical small West Texas town, its fortunes tied to the oil and gas fields that surround it. Most of the businesses either sell oil-related equipment like derricks or provide services like welding, and the night horizon is scattered with fires from the gas burn-off. You rarely see anyone on the streets, unless it's lunchtime and they're waiting outside the Best of the West hamburger stand or coming out of Martin's department store, which is smaller than most big-city markets. The streets are named after states—Texas, Mississippi, Pennsylvania—or are numbered (those don't get very high). As for the name Big Lake, you could be excused for thinking that the small reservoir at the east end of town as you enter from San Angelo is the "big lake," but the name refers to a wide, shallow basin in the dirt outside the south end that fills with water only during prolonged heavy rains, which are rarer than cool days in June. It was Big Lake that the producers of a gritty movie called *Flesh and Bone* found when they went looking for a little town that screamed rural Texas. Meg Ryan and Dennis Quaid holing up in the Mustang Motel for several weeks of filming in 1993 was about the biggest thing to happen in Big Lake in seventy years, since the Santa Rita number one blew in May of 1923, the first gusher in West Texas and the reason for the town's existence. Today the fields are worked mostly by Latino immigrants, and a lot of the students are their sons and daughters.

Finding Reagan County High wasn't hard. You enter town on the main drag and turn right. I drove around the school before parking. The buildings seemed well maintained, and of course the football stadium was in great shape. I knew even before pulling up alongside it that the baseball diamond would look more like a sandlot. Right next door were the local rodeo and the 4-H headquarters. I laughed to see that the mascot was an owl—the Reagan County High School Owls. I imagined hearing the students chant "Go, Owls" and wondered if they only played games at night. With the thermometer at about 110, it didn't seem like such a bad idea.

David Steele, the athletic director and head football coach, was a big man with a big handshake. We talked a little, he said he'd read my résumé and was impressed, and he hired me to be an assistant football coach, head baseball coach, and a teacher of integrated physics and chemistry. I signed the contract half an hour later and drove home intending to spring the news on Lorri as a kind of "Oh, by the way" surprise, but she said I was smiling like a cat with two canaries in his belly.

"I'm working," I said.

"I figured," she said. "Either that or the White Sox want you back." Pause. "Good for you, Jimmy. I'm really happy."

The job paid $32,000, about the same as Lorri's salary—and that made me happy; I wasn't a kept man anymore.

"Thirty-two," she said. "That's amazing."

I said, "Well, you should see this place. The people are really nice, that's for sure, but they have to come up with some incentive to get anybody out there. It's kind of bleak."

I said, "We can rent a three-bedroom house for three hundred and fifty dollars"—less than half what we were paying—and we began moving.

My job as assistant football coach began two days later, at seven in the morning, with the start of two-a-day practices. I left home at five-thirty. Like a jogging companion, the full moon stayed on my left shoulder all the way to Big Lake. It set on the horizon when I reached the reservoir, looking as bright as the sun but twice as big. I stopped to watch it disappear—and an owl landed on the road in front of me.

I didn't know what it meant, but I knew it meant something.

* * *

After the first week I convinced myself that I had a brain tumor. After the second week I finally mentioned something to Coach Steele. "I can't get rid of this head-ache," I said. "It's been killing me ever since I got here. Aspirin, Tylenol, Excedrin—nothing touches it."

"Don't worry," he said. "It'll go away in another week or so."

"How do you know?"

"Because everybody has it at first. It's the vapors from the gas plant out there. You get used to them, and it goes away."

I stared at him for a second and said, "You're not kidding, are you?"

He said, "Hey, that's why we're paying you the big bucks."

I said, "I thought it was to buy bottled water." He laughed. Big Lake's water supply flows from "Lake Nasty." It smells like sulfur and tastes like garbage. If there were any homeless in Big Lake they'd stand out on Second Street with signs saying, "Will work for Evian."

I rented a three-bedroom house a few blocks from school, expecting that Lorri would commute. But as the days grew shorter Lorri realized that she didn't see well enough in the dark to drive in it at least an hour a day along a road famous for deer accidents.

Of course, Hunter was already several weeks into

first grade. I thought that moving him out of Big Lake before that semester ended in December would be wrong. Until then he'd drive with me, leaving San Angelo before sunrise, while he was still asleep, and coming home at night, after his bedtime.

You didn't have to be Gordon Wood to see that *Sports Illustrated* wouldn't be featuring our football team that season. I coached the defensive backs and thought we'd be lucky to win a game. The kids appreciated that I did my job without shouting or berating. They listened well and tried hard and wanted to take what they heard and do better, and I let them know that honest effort was good enough. That set me apart from most Texas coaches as much as the way I taught science. In my integrated physics and chemistry classes, I didn't hand out worksheets and read magazines while waiting for them back. I actually explained concepts like the laws of gravity and chemical reactions in ways that made sense of them (I'd learned the lessons myself the night before). We did research in the library and conducted experiments and kept journals and wrote papers, and they tried hard. They were eager to learn. I liked them for that. I liked the school. I liked my jobs. I liked the other teachers and coaches and townspeople.

What I didn't like was waking my boy at five-something every morning and driving in the dark while he slept, and having him be the first one at school. I hated that.

One morning in October we pulled up on Mertzon, which is halfway between San Angelo and Big Lake. If Big Lake is a town, Mertzon is a gas station. You know you're there only by seeing the sign and passing the place where the highway crosses over an arroyo; we called it the Mertzon bridge. It was about six-fifteen and still dark. Hunter slept in the backseat. Headlights approached from the other direction—the tenth or twelfth other vehicle on the road that morning—and suddenly they swerved into my lane and came directly toward us. I saw a deer scamper off the road and, in my headlights, the face of the elderly woman who'd tried to avoid hitting it as she bore down on us. In those milliseconds that seemed frozen in time, the screeching of tires sounded normal, and I felt glad that Hunter wasn't awake to see the impact; he'd wake up in heaven. Would I be there to explain everything? Or was I going the other way?

We didn't collide head-on, and I can't explain why other than to credit an invisible hand for moving my Cutlass to the extreme lip of the Mertzon bridge. Her truck glanced off my left rear fender and came to rest about an inch shy of falling into the arroyo. Her engine, in fact, did fall in, as the front of her truck hung precariously on the railing. I checked on Hunter, who was still asleep, and jumped out to help her. I carefully opened her door, worried that the truck might yet tip over and in, and grabbed her shaking hand and pulled. I held her, and then she noticed Hunter in the car and started to weep.

"I could've killed him," she whimpered.

That night on the way home Hunter and I stopped at the site. Seeing it made any explanation of how we'd survived more mysterious. Her skid marks were wider than my car. We should've been dead. And I never felt more alive. The hot air rising off the asphalt smelled wonderful.

The next day I enrolled Hunter in the San Angelo school around the corner, and the day after that I had a blowout on the road at the same spot and came within a hair of going off the bridge. I wondered if someone was trying to tell me something.

Someone was. Lorri bought a home pregnancy test and came down the stairs crying. "I'm pregnant," she said.

Damn. We were still ironing out our wrinkled relationship. The last thing we needed was another mouth to feed and another logistical problem to solve.

Fourth period, right before lunch, was a workout period for the varsity football team. Wearing jeans and cowboy boots—my usual outfit—I punted the ball several times to the special teams unit, to let them practice their alignments. They needed it badly. Tomorrow was the season's final game, and we hadn't won any of the previous nine.

The bell rang to end the period. I walked to my classroom, sat at my desk, ate a sandwich, typed grades into my computer, and then the bell rang to begin fifth period. I stood—and fell. I stood again—and fell. My left foot wouldn't bear the weight. I sat on the edge of the desk and saw how the foot just dangled at the ankle. I taught my class from a seated position, and when the bell rang limped to the locker room like Quasimodo, dragging my useless foot behind me. Paul Sundre, the team trainer, ordered me to lie down and slipped my boot off. His face reminded me of the war-movie medic who opens his wounded buddy's shirt and sees the ugly damage.

"Jimmy, I'm not kidding," Paul said, staring at my swollen shin. "You have got to get to the hospital, and I mean right now."

He called the hospital in San Angelo. Coach Steele wandered in, saw the leg, and looked as if he was going to cry.

Coach Steele asked if I had a ride to the hospital. I lied.

I'd intended to drive straight there, but after a while in the car I figured that the ride was relaxing my leg, even healing it, so instead I drove home and tested my hypothesis by standing on both legs.

"You're really stupid, you know that?" I said out

loud as I fell in the doorway and dragged myself to the phone.

I called Lorri's office. She was waiting at the hospital when I pulled up. So was Dr. Ryan, the orthopedic surgeon who'd tightened my shoulder a few years before.

He rolled a pinprick device over the area, and I said I couldn't feel anything. He speculated that kicking the football with cowboy boots on had caused the shin to swell and cut off the nerve. Then he said he wasn't qualified to perform such a tricky operation and had already called in a neurological surgeon.

The surgeon sliced the shin to release the stored blood and let the nerve breathe. Three days later he sewed it up, except for a small leakage crease, and warned me to rest the leg at home for a week, but after two days in bed I started thinking about my students, who'd worked so hard in class. Most had never enjoyed science before, and I didn't want to lose that momentum; the kids might feel abandoned. Besides, I saw the way their circumstances had conspired against them. These were working-class kids who expected to inherit their parents' reality, leaving towns at midnight to chase jobs along the grapevine. What if I could do something to change what they believed in and hoped for? Stranger things had happened. To me.

The next day I showed up at school wearing sweatpants and paced in front of the class as always. In the afternoon a kid in the front row noticed my pants sticking to my leg; I was leaking again. The school nurse said I'd better rush to the hospital. I did. It was a staph infection, raging hotter by the second. The medical staff began pumping antibiotics through an IV and sticking Q-tips that long into the wound. A doctor pointed to the clock and gave the infection an hour to stop growing. If it didn't, he said, they'd have to amputate my lower leg to save my life.

I watched the clock and kept tabs on the infection, but there was no way they were taking my leg.

The hour passed and so did the threat. I graduated to the strongest oral antibiotic available, and it tore up my stomach. Nausea, not infection, kept me out of school until after Christmas vacation. I made it back before finals, around the same time the school board met and decided to purge the coaching staff. (A winless football season in Texas is nearly a hanging offense.) I think the words used to describe David Steele were "lack of football enthusiasm." The man cared more about the kids' education than their athleticism.

I was one of three coaches not fired. They figured you couldn't blame the football team's miserable season on the defensive backs' coach, and anyway they'd really hired me to coach baseball; I should be given a season to see what I could do.

David Steele's replacement as head football coach and athletic director was Scott Simpson. He was a big man, about six three and near three hundred pounds, in his late thirties. He'd played college football and coached for about fifteen years, most recently as an assistant at Mesquite High, a 5-A school (Reagan County was only 2-A) just east of Dallas. He'd never been a head coach before, and now was also athletic director. He came in with a lot of fire, anxious to prove that he deserved this big break. As I would discover, he shared a lot in common with Gordon Wood. Both were excellent football coaches. Both believed in shouting at players. And both thought baseball was the Antichrist.

I'd spent much of the football season recruiting players, talking to them about the greatest game in the world. They were skeptical at first. Baseball season overlapped basketball season for a few weeks, and basketball is a mania. But my playing professionally once upon a time gave me credibility. So did my popularity in the classroom and mild manner on the field. So did my basketball skills. The kids shook their heads at the way I handled the ball and buried jump shots; at thirty-four, I could've been the school's starting point guard.

But everything would buy nothing if I didn't transform that junkyard into a garden.

Reagan High's baseball field looked like an abandoned tract gone to seed. Occasional clusters of dead grass poked out of the gravel infield and outfield. You could hurt yourself running, and you'd better not fall or slide. It was no wonder the previous baseball coach had had to beg for players in the stands. The field said everything the kids needed to know about the school's opinion of baseball. They were Texans, not 1930s New Yorkers pitching rocks on sandlots in the snow. In Texas, baseball's not considered the national pastime. You have to coax kids to play. My attitude was that appearances are important. I believed that if I built it, they would come.

I called baseball coaches and ground crewsmen and horticulturists, and bought bags of seed and tools. And I got down on my hands and knees and started pulling weeds and planting seed and watering every square inch. It was a huge job. I was lucky that the high school was right above a thriving well; it cost nothing to run the big hoses as much as I wanted. The hard part was dragging them where they needed to be.

A lot of people stopped to watch for a few minutes or called out to ask what I was doing. One day a tall, lanky kid pulled up alongside the field, in the vacant area near the 4-H center. He stepped out of his truck and yelled, "Hey, need some help?"

I said sure, and he kicked off his boots and came over barefoot. His name was Neil. He'd played baseball here for two years and graduated the previous June.

"This field's never looked like anything good," he said, and I told him there was a new sheriff in town. From then on he showed up after work whenever he could, to help me. He said, "You'd have a lot more help if this was the football field."

I said, "I wouldn't need it."

By the first day of practice the grass was as green as the football field. Forty-five kids showed up to play—five times the number that had come out a year before.

I felt like a lottery winner until one of the other coaches came over specifically to tell me the kids were slackers with bad attitudes. "They'll never do what you tell them to do," he said. "You'll see."

I disagreed. My sense was that the kids would listen to the message if the messenger didn't yell. They'd been screamed at by football and basketball and track coaches so often that they'd become deaf to loud voices. Mine was quiet.

And they did listen. They listened to me tell them they were good. They weren't—but why did they need to hear that? What they needed was encouragement. Everybody does. You have to believe you're a winner to be a winner.

I kept thirty of the forty-five kids, dividing them between varsity and junior varsity teams. The JVs were there to learn; the varsity had to learn on the job, with the stakes high: Reagan County High's baseball future and, maybe, my job.

Some of the kids were talented but had never

played. With a single practice field for both teams, I'd send everyone out to their positions and have the older guys teach the younger guys as much as they could. My assistant coach worked with the outfielders, while I took the infielders. We worked on pitching and hitting and fielding and all the elements of baseball that take a lifetime to learn; in its way it's as intricate and interesting a game as chess. And there's nothing harder in sports than hitting a baseball, which is why we spent so much time on batting practice. I figured that the best place to judge their swings and make corrective comments was from the pitcher's mound, so I did the pitching.

"Coach, you're too fast," they moaned. "Are you trying to kill us?"

I laughed off their complaints, thinking I couldn't have been throwing any faster than the average high school pitcher, then reared back and threw harder. They obviously needed the practice.

I cheered them on and flattered them and taught them as much how to win as how to play. And they began winning. It surprised them until we entered a tournament in Sonora, a hundred miles southeast, and made the tournament finals, losing only six to five against Ballinger, a 3-A school that had an excellent team. On the bus ride home, the team was buzzed. We'd now played ten games, losing only three.

"Hey, we *are* pretty good, Coach," somebody said.

The kids talked about winning the district championship and making the state tournament and even being state champs. It was heady talk and ridiculously unrealistic for a ragtag bunch of rookies, but they weren't going to hear a discouraging word from me. I drove the bus and listened to them whoop and holler in the back.

Too bad things weren't as warm at home as they were at school. Lorri's pregnancy had come at a delicate time in our relationship and rocked our world. It was like a bright flashlight shining through cracks in a wall, making them more visible. We hadn't repaired those cracks before living together again; we'd begun living together again because we intended to repair them. But there were so many, and all of them seemed to grow bigger with Lorri's belly, and we never seemed to have enough time. Lorri came home late, and I came home later and then had to go over my lesson plan or coaching strategies before bed. Those silences—being in the same room without talking about the dead elephant on the floor—drove even me crazy. And what little free time we had was spent doing errands. At least we were making ends meet. That kept money from being the catalyst for fights and deceiving us into thinking that we were fighting about money.

What we needed was time together. I asked Lorri to come watch a baseball game and promised that we'd both be home before dark. I wanted to see her and wanted her to see me succeed at something. She agreed to leave work early one day and drive out to Big Lake. It was fun to turn around from the dugout every now and then and look at her sitting among the thirty or forty other people in the stands (four times more than the previous year). She'd smile, and I'd smile, and we won the game. I drove behind her on the way back, and when we walked in the house she said her leg felt damp. What if her water had broken? She was only six months pregnant. She checked herself in the bathroom and looked worried. The only thing more frightening than having another child was losing the child.

"I think I better go to the hospital," she said.

I made dinner for the kids and put them to bed. Lorri came in around nine. The lab tests had said that the liquid was not amniotic fluid. We went to sleep and she woke me in the middle of the night. The bed was wet. We called her mother to come stay with the kids and hurried to the hospital. Now the tests showed that the liquid was definitely amniotic fluid.

"We don't have neonatal facilities here," the doctor said. "We're sending you to Harris Methodist Hospital in Fort Worth."

But not in a car; that would have taken at least four hours. In an air ambulance.

They shot Lorri with something to repress labor and something to calm her, and put her in an ambulance for the ride to the airport. I climbed in behind the two paramedics. We rode with the siren on and pulled onto the tarmac next to the tiny twin-engine plane. I wondered how they were going to fit Lorri in, let alone the rest of us.

Lorri didn't mind being strapped down. Those drugs had made her happy; she was flying even before we took off. The paramedics knelt beside her and attached the IV. The only space for me was in the very back, in an area usually reserved for small cargo. I wedged myself in, like a fifteen-and-a-half-foot truck under a fifteen-foot bridge. There was no need for a seat belt or a strap. If the plane had crashed, they'd have found me upside down in the same space. In fact, the plane nearly did crash. It approached the Fort Worth airport and banked sideways for a long way as it came down. I thought the bottom wing was going to hit the ground. So did the paramedics. Their faces looked as terrified as mine must have.

The staff obstetrician said the baby—a girl, the tests showed—was too small to deliver. Lorri would have to take special drugs and lie flat on her back, except for going to the bathroom and two quick trips a day around the corridor in a wheelchair.

"For how long?" I asked.

"Let's put it this way," he said. "We don't want that baby coming down the chute for three months, if we can help it. Every day we hold her off is important."

My choice was either to go back to San Angelo and

Big Lake, or to stay with Lorri. It was no choice. I arranged for her mom to take care of the kids so I could stay. I think Lorri was surprised.

Did someone say we needed time? Now we had it. Nothing but time. Time to talk and to argue and to make up, and no time for excuses.

Lorri and I had loved each other for fifteen years without really being on the same wavelength. We'd liked each other first and then loved each other without understanding marriage and what it takes to become part of something that's bigger than you and your will and your need to be right. Love isn't enough. But love had kept us going through all the years of running uphill and wondering why the climb was so hard. It was almost like knowing the answer to a riddle without knowing the question. Everything seemed backward. Even when we were apart and I felt my life had stopped, the only person I really wanted to talk to about it was Lorri.

What went on between us in that hospital room over the following weeks had nothing to do with miracles or magic or mystery. We talked and sat silently and played cards and laughed and napped and read and watched television and ate carrot cake that I bought at the cafeteria downstairs, and in just living without a schedule or obligations to everyone but each other we discovered that we hadn't wasted all those years.

Big emotional climaxes, I learned, don't have to

come in the rain with music swelling. I'd just brought Lorri back to the room after her five-minute wheel-chair break, and sat down next to her on the bed. We were playing Go Fish and I'd asked for any eights and she told me to go fish. Instead of searching through the deck I cupped her hands in mine.

"I love you," I said. It was a statement years in the making.

"I know," she said. Somehow, that seemed more important than what came next: "I love you, too."

I said, "I know you do," and wondered whether feeling loved, not loving, was what had been missing.

We hugged and cried and talked about the separation and what had led up to it and why we'd been brought back together and how this baby was a sign that we were supposed to stay together. Then we argued for five weeks about what to name her, finally settling on Jamie.

Mom and Charles drove my car up to Fort Worth so that I could drive back now and then to pick up test papers and my grade book, and they brought Hunter and Jessica a few times for visits. I kept in contact with the baseball team. It was being managed by my assistant coach, Bo Comacho, a big, hard-nosed Latino with a master's degree who'd played linebacker in college and had the Texas coach's mentality. My kids, mostly Latinos themselves, didn't take to his manner and lost most of the rest of the games that season. I felt bad for the way their high hopes had crashed, but there was always next year.

Jamie showed her personality early by fighting the drugs the doctors gave Lorri and coming six weeks early. She weighed only four pounds and spent the first week of her life in an incubator (like me). I didn't know four pounds could be so small until Charles reached out to touch her and she disappeared beneath his gloved hand. But she was beautiful—blond hair and blue eyes with a light behind them. You could already see that she was blessed with confidence.

Lorri and I drove home to San Angelo, with Jamie in the back, believing that we'd never have to climb uphill again.

It was the first morning of football two-a-days in August. I left home in the dark to be there at seven and put a cassette I'd just bought into the tape player— music by the Kinleys. Over and over, all the way to Big Lake, I rewound and played the same song, the theme to *Touched by an Angel.* "Everybody needs hope / Some kind of peace of mind they can call their own / I believe that somebody's out there watching / Somebody's out there watching . . ."

Coach Simpson had made me the quarterback coach. We weren't half an hour into the first drills when he stopped the action and shouted at me in front of the players:

"Are you trying to sabotage this program?"

"Excuse me?"

"What do you think you're doing?"

"The drill," I said.

"You're not running it right! I'll show you—again! How many times am I going to have to?!"

You needed a micrometer to measure his allowable margin of error. Whatever I did was wrong. Time after time. Nothing satisfied him. And every criticism was loud and public. Apparently the man was incapable of speaking without exclamation marks. By the end of practice I felt wrung out. Dinner was chocolate milk and Rolaids. The next night, after the same kind of day, my Rolaids chaser was a couple of beers.

Coach Simpson and I must have been Captain Bligh and Fletcher Christian in a previous life. I can't think of another explanation for our relationship. The season for me was a series of harangues. If a linebacker missed a tackle, it was my fault. If a receiver dropped a ball, it was the quarterback's fault and therefore my fault. If the laundry didn't dry in time, it was my fault.

"You know why I get on you, don't you?" he asked one afternoon. "It's because the kids like you so much. They see me do it, it makes 'em play that much harder."

I didn't believe that and told him he'd miscalculated, and he told me I'd never amount to anything as a coach. "You're too nice," he said. "Kids don't respect that."

I guess you can't argue with success. In one season, the team went from zero wins to six wins. Simpson was rightfully proud.

So was I. I'd taken a second-string JV quarterback and in one season made him into a second-team all-district varsity starter.

The season ended with a loss in the first round of the district playoffs. No one had expected us to go that far. The players felt they'd won a moral victory, and anyway basketball started soon. When you watched that team practice, you knew they might play themselves into a championship.

In the meantime, I had a baseball diamond to prepare. It wasn't easy. For some reason, much of the equipment seemed to be locked in sheds for which there were no keys, and requisition requests seemed to get lost without being filled. I didn't understand why and confronted Simpson, threatening to take my complaints to the school board. He said I didn't know what kind of trouble I was making for myself and told me I had blinders on—"You only see small things, not big problems." I said I'd learned to take care of big problems by solving small problems.

It came to the point where I got mad just looking at Simpson. He suggested that we take our feud outside and settle it once and for all. That would not have been in the best interest of my face. The only way for me to win the fight that I didn't want to fight in the first place was by succeeding.

I borrowed equipment and asked a local store to donate paint for the outfield fence, and after it had a new coat of blue, the school nurse, Mary Kay Cockrell, who's an artist, volunteered to draw a large owl on it. I planted annual grass and had help nurturing it to life. Neil, the young man who'd come by the previous year, worked on it every day with me. So did his friend David, a former football player who'd just moved back to Big Lake. We cut the grass with an old-fashioned hand lawn mower and babied the infield with tweezers and scissors. Some nights we worked till eleven-thirty, under the lights. Some nights Neil set his alarm for midnight and came to turn off the water. The resurrection of the baseball field was the talk of Big Lake. People pulled into the parking lot to see for themselves. It looked as proud as the football stadium.

Every player but the three who'd graduated returned from the 1998 team and were joined by thirteen new players. That gave me fifty-five (a total not far below the football team's), of whom fifteen were legitimate varsity baseball players. I drove to work every morning listening to the Kinleys—"Everybody needs hope"—and imagining what winning a championship might do for these kids. I believed it could be life-changing.

Texas high school baseball begins officially in early February. But a third of my varsity were still playing basketball. The team had cruised through the regular season and stood a good chance of making it to the state championship game. I canceled a couple of exhibition baseball tournaments, thinking it wasn't good for the confidence of my JVs to be thrown into the coliseum without weapons and eaten by veteran lions. We'd just have to wait for basketball season to end and in the meantime keep practicing.

The basketball coaches looked over the pairings and figured that the team's first-round opponent would be its toughest competition until the championship, and it was a fun game to watch. With fifty seconds remaining, we led by six points. Then a bad foul call, a bad shot, a bad pass, and four clutch baskets left our players lying on the court, wondering what the hell had happened. What happened is that they'd given up eight points in less than a minute, and lost by two.

The whole school suffered from the same colossal hangover. This championship had been theirs for the taking and then snatched away. It wasn't fair; they cheated; the refs were paid off; we never catch a break—the kids came up with more conspiracy theories than Oliver Stone. I waited a few days for the depression to pass. But it didn't. Two weeks later my players were still sleepwalking through baseball practice. They wandered like zombies, letting pop flies drop between them and swinging two beats too late at fastballs that were unhittably out of the strike zone anyway. Worse, they whined constantly, daydreamed in class, and walked around school with their heads down, acting beaten.

"Look," I said, "you all had a great football season. In basketball, if you hadn't lost on a fluke call, you would've gone to the state championships. Things didn't go your way. So that's done now. Let's just shake it off and move on to the next sport."

But they wouldn't, and with the season beginning soon I started to panic a little. Hunter's Little League team could've given my guys a good game.

I bore down in practice, making them hit my best fastball. All they did was complain about how fast I was throwing. Then I let them throw to me and sent pitch after pitch bouncing off the little house far behind the right field fence, about 450 feet away. They loved watching the balls fly as much as I loved hitting them, and I challenged them to do the same against me—make practice fun. We were, after all, playing a game. But for them this was about winning now, and they were too hurt to believe they could overcome the odds and conspiracies and win again.

The time had come for my Knute Rockne pep talk.

I didn't have a Knute Rockne pep talk.

*　　*　　*

It was a late afternoon at the beginning of March. The days weren't yet as long as the shadows. We'd finished practicing and dragged the irrigation pipes onto the outfield for watering. Then we gathered near the left field stands, in front of the little hut where we stored our gear. They sat on the grass. I stood quietly for a minute, and we all watched the water shoot from the pipe holes on the other side.

"The thing that worries me," I began, "is that I can't shake you guys out of this lackadaisical attitude. And I don't know if it's me; maybe I'm doing something wrong and can't reach you. Or maybe it's you. Or maybe it's the combination."

Now I had their attention.

"What you better start realizing," I said, "is that it takes dreams to accomplish anything. You have to have dreams. Without dreams, you're nothing in this world. You need them. And the bigger your dreams, the more you can accomplish, the more you can do, the farther you'll go."

I didn't know where any of this was coming from. I just opened my mouth and let my lips flap and heard the words for the first time as they were said. Somewhere in me there's a romantic soul that wanted these mostly Latino kids, the sons of immigrants, to appreciate the American Dream and trust they could live it. They needed inspiration.

"Reach out!" I said. "Put a dream or goal just past

where you can touch it at that moment. Then, once you do touch it, you've gotta reach a little higher. And a little bit higher. And a little bit higher. That's how you get better, no matter what you do in life."

I stood on that pulpit for a while and spouted every platitude I'd ever heard, and when I finished there was silence, but not the awed kind. It was finally broken by Joel DeLaGarza, my senior catcher and chemistry classroom aide, the kind of shy and polite and earnest kid you never see in movies.

"What about you, Coach?" he said. "You're preaching one thing and doing another." He paused. Now he had *my* attention. I looked into the other faces, wondering if they knew what he meant.

"Don't get me wrong," Joel said. "We all love you a lot. But the way you can throw the baseball"— pause—"why aren't you still playing?"

A chorus of voices agreed.

I laughed. But not at them. It was an embarrassed laugh. Their question had nothing to do with my arm and everything to do with how they felt about me. They saw me through their hearts, as better than I really was. What other explanation could there be? Looking at my face they could not have noticed the pain of some unrealized dream. I was thirty-five years old and at peace—married to a wonderful woman; father to three great kids; lucky to get paid for doing something that excited me. The way I understood my life and its disappointments was that I fit into some sort of divine plan. Instead of pitching in the major leagues, I was supposed to make a difference in the lives of these kids. And I loved doing it, believing that that's what God wanted me to be doing. The road had been too long and winding, with too many detours that led onto more scenic roads, for there to be any other explanation. In my mind, I had it all.

But they must have seen something in me I couldn't see in myself.

"Why are you laughing?" someone asked. I couldn't tell who said it, with all the chattering, and I stopped laughing. They were really serious.

Joel's voice stood out again. "If we win district, Coach," he said, "you have to try out for a major-league team."

I suppose my eyes widened in surprise. The idea of a thirty-five-year-old gray-hair showing up at a major-league tryout camp to compete against kids young enough to be his sons is funnier than anything Jerry Seinfeld ever said and more preposterous than all of Mother Goose.

But why did they have to know that? Aren't dreams sometimes built on naïve ideas? What good would be served by telling them that some dreams are disguised nightmares?

Reality was not what I wanted to sell. Hope was.

Theirs was an offer I couldn't refuse. Not for my

sake, but for theirs. They would now be playing for something that forced them to dream bigger and reach higher, beyond themselves. Reagan County High had never before won the district championship. The goal lay just beyond their grasp. They'd have to work harder than ever.

The perfect plan had fallen in my lap. If it took a fairy tale to light a fire under them, I'd gladly strike the match.

My players hated to see Coach Simpson lash out at me, and on the ancient theory that "the enemy of my enemy is my friend," they began warming to Bo, my assistant coach, when Simpson's choice words perforated him a few times. They believed Simpson intended to eliminate baseball and fire me and that he was jealous of my popularity. More than the bet, which no one mentioned all season, our common feelings toward Simpson helped to unify us. So did the three- and four-hour rides to West Texas towns you've never heard of in a bus that groaned at fifty miles an hour. There were closer high schools, but most of them considered baseball a useless rival to football, track, and basketball. Isn't that what Simpson thought?

Our practices were like parties with a purpose. We had fun and kept focused. I worked with the pitchers as much on composure as on mechanics. "It's important that you don't let anybody see what you're really feeling," I said. "If they ever think they can get to you, then you're done. If they ever get in your head, they'll never let up."

Rudy, my best pitcher, said, "If they ever get in my head, they won't know what to think."

I pitched batting practice until my arm ached, throwing harder the louder they complained about the speed, then tossing an unannounced slow curve in to keep them honest. All the work paid off. They developed quick reflexes and bats, and the team improved every game and took on a personality just short of cocky. They believed in themselves even when they fell behind, winning most games by several runs and all of them by at least one.

One game remained on the schedule, one obstacle between them and the district championship.

Van Horn High School is in a small mining town about 250 miles west of Big Lake. Its kids probably have a lot in common with Big Lake's, and who knows, maybe something important was riding on this game's outcome for them, too. I remember hearing before the season about Van Horn's ace pitcher, a kid with a nasty slider to back up his nasty fastball, and thinking that if he were half as good as the gossip, the rest of the district would be playing for second place.

We played the final game halfway between Big Lake and Van Horn, on a field in Fort Stockton. The coun-

tryside is harsh. Few of the dead buried in the ceme-
tery that dates back to the town's founding, 150 years
ago, lived to be forty. I was so nervous before the game,
I almost didn't either.

It was hot there, even at six o'clock, and the low sun
was especially cruel to players on the right side. That
handicap should have affected both teams, but when
the sun was at its worst in the first innings, we couldn't
seem to hit the ball at all, so their second baseman, first
baseman, and right fielder didn't have to contend with
being blinded. Meanwhile, their batters swung late at
Rudy's fastball and hit an unusual number of pop-ups
and ground balls to second base. Joaquin ("Whack"),
our second baseman, would normally have caught
them all. But the mitt he'd used since Little League had
crumbled a few days before, and he was using a new
one, giving him two good reasons for making errors
that cost us three runs.

We were behind three to one when we came to bat
in the top of the fifth. I saw something in their pitcher's
delivery that said he was tiring, and I told my guys to
be aggressive. The first two batters singled, and
Whack doubled them both home. Now the score was
tied, and we knew and they knew that this game was
ours. Kellen surprised them with a bunt single, Joe
David hit a triple off the green wall, Joel doubled, three
or four more hits followed, Van Horn changed pitch-

ers, we scored seven runs, and the fat lady began warming up her vocal cords.

By the bottom of the last inning the sun had set and the stadium lights were turned on. I wasn't sure which was worse on the eyes. With two outs, a batter hit a pop-up to second base. Whack caught it with two hands, and my kids rushed into a heap near the mound. World Series winners aren't as excited as these kids were. They jumped around and hugged everyone in sight and shouted "We did it!" Most of them cried through their laughter. I hung back in the dugout and snapped off two rolls of photos and just savored the moment— *their* moment.

The thought that I now had to uphold my part of some agreement never entered my mind.

What did occur to me as I sat in the driver's seat of the bus, waiting for my players to exit the locker room, was that I would not be their coach next year. Texas allows you three years on an emergency teaching certificate, and this had been my third year. The fault was mine for not earning it earlier. True, I'd enrolled in an intensive six-week program that began in July and would have my permanent certificate by the end of the summer, and the Reagan County principal had asked me to remain as a science teacher in the fall. But Simpson had already hired my coaching replacement, and staying on only to teach would've hurt too much.

Besides, Simpson's dislike of me seemed to be another of those mysterious forces guiding my destiny. Lorri had always wanted to live in a big city, and now she and I and the kids were moving to Fort Worth. There are a dozen colleges in the area, and she had job leads at all of them. Me, I had a coaching and teaching job waiting at a 4-A school. We had so much to look forward to. What I hoped for now was that this season would somehow make a difference forever in the lives of these kids.

What my players didn't know was that I planned to take them out for steaks before making the three-hour drive home. What I didn't know is that they'd been rehearsing this moment all season.

One by one they lined up outside the bus. I wondered why they didn't all just pile in.

Joel was the first to board. Stopping just to my right, he looked me dead in the eye and said, "Our part of the bargain is done. Now you do *your* part." He walked to the rear of the bus, and Rudy boarded next.

"You gotta try out now, Coach," he said.

Matt followed. "A deal's a deal."

Then Whack: "We did it. You have to, too."

And so it went, player by player, until the entire team had filed past me with a remark.

"Okay," I said.

That's all I had to say. I'm a man who does what he

says he's going to do, no matter how ridiculous it is. And it was ridiculous, the thought of my finding an open tryout camp somewhere and embarrassing myself in front of major-league scouts.

We stopped at the restaurant, and I asked Bo to take the kids in while I stayed outside and called the appropriate newspapers and TV stations with the news that the Reagan County High School Owls had made history by winning their first district championship. The calls took a while. By the time I walked into the restaurant, some of the kids already had food in front of them. But no one ate. All faces turned to me. Several of the boys had wet eyes.

I did, too, after they handed me the game ball, signed by each of them.

I said, "Thank you." I hope I said it in a way that told the whole story.

The playoffs began the following week with a best-of-three series. We won the first game, lost the second in the bottom of the seventh, then fell apart completely in the last game. Our championship season had ended, but the team cried more out of happiness than disappointment. They had accomplished the impossible and felt like winners. The boys who hugged me that day said how happy they'd been to play for me—I'd believed in them—and to hurry up and try out. I promised I would.

* * *

It was mid-June now. I'd been out of school for three weeks and spent every day with my children. Hunter was nearly nine now, Jessica was five, and Jamie had just turned one. They were growing fast. I couldn't remember feeling as content. We enjoyed each other so much I hated not having the whole summer to do this, but the teaching certification class was beginning in a few weeks. My only real concern was this tryout business. I had to get it over with sometime.

A short item in the San Angelo newspaper said that several teams would be holding a joint open tryout at Dallas Baptist University on June 19. That was a Saturday. I figured I'd wake up early, leave the kids with Lorri, drive the four hours there, get laughed out of the stadium, drive home, call the boys in Big Lake to say I'd kept my end of the bargain, and drop into bed. Done. End of subject. Move on with life.

The Monday before that Saturday, I took Hunter and Jessica and Jamie to visit my dad in Brownwood. As I pulled into Dad's driveway, a local radio announcer mentioned another open tryout, this one for the Tampa Bay Devil Rays; it was also being held on the nineteenth, but right there in Brownwood, at Howard Payne University. The announcer explained that the Devil Rays were looking for prospects between the ages of eighteen and twenty-four. I laughed, knowing that a thirty-five-year-old wouldn't be welcome in Dallas, either.

That night Lorri told me she'd been asked to administer an admissions test on Saturday. She couldn't watch the kids that day. Neither could her mother, who'd just broken her ankle. It was up to me to take care of them. Did I want to wake them at three in the morning to be in Dallas by eight? Or spend the night with them in a Dallas hotel? No. Not when the Devil Rays were having a tryout that same day, almost in my backyard. At first I felt a little guilty. But why? The Devil Rays were a major-league team. I'd still be keeping my word.

On Saturday morning I put the kids in the car and headed for Howard Payne. Hunter sat shotgun, Jessica and Jamie in back. I'd asked Dad and Teresa to meet me there later and watch the kids.

As soon as I drove under the Truman Harlow overpass and crossed the train tracks and drove into the gravel parking lot on the left field line and parked by the electrical building, I felt queasy. Crowded around the redbrick fieldhouse that says "HPU Baseball" were dozens of boys who really did, as a matter of fact, look young enough to be my sons. I calculated that most of them were still in diapers when I played here, and noticed that all of them now wore regulation baseball pants and shirts. Then I glanced down at my own shorts and T-shirt. As George Gobel used to say, I felt like a pair of brown shoes in a world of tuxedoes.

"Hunter, what have I done to myself?" I asked. It was a rhetorical question.

"You made a promise, Dad," he answered. "You may as well get out of the car."

I almost asked him how he'd gotten so smart, but he'd probably have had an answer for that, too.

From the trunk I retrieved my glove, some softball pants I'd worn a few seasons back, and a pair of ten-year-old cleats that hurt my feet. Jessica held Hunter's hand, he held one of mine, and with the other I pushed Jamie in her stroller across the parking lot toward the fieldhouse. We took our place in one of the two lines that snaked inside and ended at long tables. Behind each was a man, helping the boys sign up. It got to be my turn.

The potbellied man wearing a Tampa Bay cap and jacket over jeans and tennis shoes looked to be in his sixties. He was the only other guy there with white hair. His name was Doug Gassaway, one of the Devil Rays' scouts. He glanced up at me, then down at Hunter and the two girls, then back at me before smiling.

"Bringing the kids to try out?" he asked.

I quietly explained how I'd come to be there and why I needed to keep my word. He listened politely and said he didn't have time for stuff like this, not with seventy real prospects to try out, but when I promised to go quickly, he said he'd let me throw last so that I could return home with a clear conscience. Almost as an afterthought, he handed me the forms to fill out, and I thanked him.

Not until I put on the softball pants did I remember that I'd last worn them two seasons back, before losing twenty-five of the fifty pounds I'd gained in Haskell. Even with that extra twenty-five around my middle, they were huge on me. I borrowed a belt to hold them up and looked like the late Payne Stewart but without the golf clubs.

Dad and Teresa showed up and kept the kids in the stands with them. They tried to find some shade. It was 104 degrees.

I walked onto the field and saw the seventy prospects lined up to run sixty-yard dashes for time. "Are you gonna go?" a coach asked me. I shook my head. I said I was there to do one thing only: pitch.

Next they auditioned fielding skills. Infielders took ground balls and threw to first. Outfielders caught fungo flies and threw to the bases.

Then came pitching.

Each pitcher threw thirty pitches to a catcher who crouched behind home plate inside the portable batting-practice backstop. Doug Gassaway stood a little off to the side and shouted what kind of pitch he wanted to see thrown while pointing a radar gun for a speed reading.

I was the seventh and last pitcher. That gave me the chance to admire everyone else. They looked good enough to start the seventh game of the World Series. Me, I'd be the batboy. There was no doubt I'd soon be embarrassing myself, but I wasn't nervous and couldn't stop chuckling about it. I remembered once reading about a school principal who'd promised to eat live worms if his students read a certain number of books, and they did, and he had to, and now I was going to eat some worms for my kids.

Gassaway called my name and I walked to the mound, waving at Hunter and Jessica in the stands next to the third-base dugout. I stared at the catcher. He seemed so far away. I prayed that my first pitch would at least get to him without bouncing. I'd only played a couple minutes of catch and wasn't properly warmed up. No matter. I let fly anyway.

The catcher caught the ball. It was a strike, thank God. I saw Doug shake his radar gun. Apparently, the pitch had gone too slow even to register. He sent an aide into the dugout for another gun. The aide ran back and now there were two radar guns pointed at me. Doug called fastball again, I pitched, and they compared radar readings.

After the third pitch, some of the other prospects began congregating behind the backstop to watch. There had to be a reason why. But I refused to let myself think that I was doing well. That would have been too improbable. More likely they were amazed that the old guy wasn't bouncing any pitches. I was a curiosity, nothing more.

Doug called out the pitches and my arm warmed up. By the thirtieth pitch, all sixty-nine other guys were standing behind the backstop, watching—and cheering. After the fiftieth pitch—twenty more than anyone else—Doug told me that was enough.

I walked off the mound to applause.

"Jeez," he yelled out, "I wish you were ten years younger."

I laughed. "Don't we all," I said.

One of the other pitchers ran up to me. "You were throwing ninety-eight," he said breathlessly, as if I'd just turned water to wine. "Faster, sometimes."

"Baloney," I said. Ninety-eight miles an hour was Nolan Ryan territory—and much faster than I'd thrown back when, three arm surgeries and fifteen years ago.

"No, really," he insisted. "You were."

I said something must be wrong with the radar, but Doug assured me that both guns had registered the same readings. It didn't matter anyway. Honestly. I'd done what I said I was going to do, and I didn't need to do more. So I kept walking.

"Wait," Doug said. "I'm gonna call this in, and they're gonna think I'm crazy—a thirty-five-year-old throwing that hard."

"Look," I said, "I just came out here to satisfy an agreement. Thanks for letting me throw. I really appreciate it. But I'm going home."

Mission accomplished.

I loaded the kids in the car and drove to San Angelo without giving the matter five minutes of thought. I was just glad that the burden had been lifted from my shoulders.

By the time we walked into the house, my answering machine had a dozen messages from the Devil Rays, each one more eager than the last. The last caller had been Dan Jennings, the Tampa Bay scouting director.

"We want you," he said. "When can you start playing?"

CHAPTER NINE

LORRI CAME HOME that night and saw "13" in the phone message window. "What's this?" she asked.

I said, "We need to talk."

Her face dropped. I pursed my lips.

She said, "What do you mean?"

"I threw well," I said.

"I knew you would," she said.

"No," I said, "I threw really well." Pause. "We need to talk."

Listening to the messages had roused my sleeping dream. It must have showed on my face. Lorri stared at me as though I'd become Mr. Hyde again. I could see

her mind working, wondering if we were about to fall
down that hole again, the one that had taken us fifteen
years to climb out of.

"Don't you know how old you are?"

"Yeah."

"And you have a wife and three kids, right?"

"Yeah, I do."

"And you want to do what?!"

The phone rang. Lorri snatched it, said hello, listened for a moment, carried it into the bedroom, and
closed the door. I assumed the caller was from Tampa
Bay, but I didn't put my ear to the wall. Twenty minutes passed. I played with the kids. Maybe the call had
nothing to do with me. Maybe it was about work.

The bedroom door opened and Lorri said, "We need
to talk."

I said all right and sat on the bed next to her.

She said, "That was someone from the Devil Rays.
He asked a lot of questions about our family and
whether we're prepared for you to pursue a career in
baseball again, because you'd have to be gone. He
wanted to know if our family was strong enough to
stay together."

"What did you tell him?" I asked.

"Look, Jimmy," she said, "the last thing I want to
see is you getting hurt again, and I don't mean your
arm. You've been going from one job to anoth—"

Hunter and Jessica started to hit each other. I separated them and lifted Jamie off the floor. She grabbed my nose.

Lorri was right. We'd never been closer to easy street, and now I wanted to detour onto unpaved roads. No one my age who'd been out of baseball for ten years had ever played in the majors. It was impossible. But if I did rush off to try, I'd miss the certificate class and lose the Fort Worth job and—when I failed—be sacrificing our well-being. No certificate, no job. No job, no money. No money, no harmony. The cycle would start all over, and you could probably have drawn up the divorce papers. No, baseball had always been poison for me. The risk was too great and the chances too small. Lorri was right.

She said, "It's summertime and you're kind of between jobs anyway. This may be your last chance, and I don't think it'd be coming up again if it weren't supposed to happen."

"What are you saying?" Did I misunderstand?

"If you want to do this, I'll support you."

"You will?" I suddenly became that seven-year-old who was invited to play with the big boys in Key West.

She said, "Just please make sure of your decision."

I said, "I think I'm supposed to do this."

Dan Jennings had told Lorri that he'd call Sunday morning for our decision. We made dinner and ate with the kids and watched some TV. I tried not to think about the time passing and managed to fall asleep. The phone rang at first light. I jumped out of bed and answered before the first ring died. Doug Gassaway was calling from his home in Dallas.

"I want to do it," I said.

"Okay," he said, "I'll call you in a little bit with the plane information."

My God, this was really happening.

An hour later he called back and said, "Listen, they're not sure yet. They want you to come back tomorrow and see if you can throw like you threw yesterday."

It was the smart move. You don't sign a man my age who has a history of arm trouble after seeing him pitch only once. Maybe those fifty were all I had. I said, "That's fine with me," and we agreed to meet in Brownwood at noon the next day. I needed to know the truth more than he did. Could I really make it?

Monday morning broke cloudy and threatened rain over San Angelo. The kids and I drove to Brownwood. It was hot, a hundred degrees, and I could smell the rain coming. We pulled into the parking lot fifteen minutes early. Dad was already there with Teresa, talking to Doug. But the Howard Payne catcher wasn't. Doug said he'd gone off to lunch with some HPU recruits. The HPU pitching coach drove up and said he didn't know when they'd be back. We waited and waited and it started to rain. We took shelter under the dugout roof, hoping the rain would stop and the catcher would show. After half an hour the pitcher's mound was a swamp. The head coach said we could use the practice mound near the third-base dugout, which had a tarp over it, and he offered to play catcher. I windmilled my arm a few times to loosen it as he strapped on the protective equipment. We dragged the tarp off the mound and Doug retrieved a bag of new baseballs. Teresa kept the kids under an overhang by the fence. Doug stood near me, Dad close enough behind him to watch the radar gun readings. I threw the first pitch and Doug tossed me a dry ball. I threw the second and Doug tossed me a dry ball. And so it went. By the tenth pitch, I was falling off the muddy mound and sliding in the mud, but none of the fifty pitches came in slower than ninety-six miles an hour.

"That's enough," Doug said. "I have to make a call. Let's go inside."

We walked into the fieldhouse, and Doug used the phone. He talked in private for a while before putting me on with Dan Jennings. Jennings asked if I'd really thought this out. I said no, and we hung up.

Doug explained the plan. I'd be leaving on Wednesday morning for the Devil Rays' spring training facility in St. Petersburg, Florida, to get in shape. (He glanced at my stomach but was polite enough not to call me a fat tub of goo.) There would be no bonus and no salary for those weeks, just expenses and a per diem, and if I survived the camp I'd be sent to the team's double-A affiliate, in Orlando, and earn $1,500 a month. The rest was up to me and my performance. He handed me my ticket and wished me luck.

I said goodbye to Dad, knowing I might not see him for a while but thinking I might be back in a week. No one would have to tell me I was failing. I'd know before anyone and fire myself, maybe in time to take the certification class and keep the Fort Worth job.

Lorri wasn't home yet. I searched the garage for my beat-up suitcase and other baseball glove. When she came in, she didn't have to ask how it went. "I guess this is supposed to happen," she said, and we spent that night and the next day wondering why.

She drove me early Wednesday morning to the San Angelo airport. Our kids sat in back. They saw Mommy crying and reckoned this was a sad time. At the terminal we stood next to the car. Hunter stared down at the ground. Jessica clutched my leg. Jamie held Lorri's hand as tears rolled down her cheeks. I said, "I'll call you guys tonight. Okay?" Lorri and I hugged, and I walked inside. Part of me refused to believe I'd be gone longer than a week.

The flight from San Angelo to Dallas lasted an hour. I felt stupid. How could I walk away from my family to pursue a kid's dream? Before changing planes, I called Lorri at work. She said, "Are you okay? Can you do this?"

I said, "I don't know, but I'll find out."

Three and a half hours later I stepped off the plane in Tampa and was approached by a young man wearing a Devil Rays T-shirt. He introduced himself as Tom Moore and we piled my bags into the back of his subcompact and drove straight to the Rays' spring training facility. Tom Foley, the director of minor-league operations, set me up with workout gear and sent me outside into the wet June heat. My catcher was a young guy rehabbing an injury. Foley held a radar gun on me. I threw in the low nineties and showed him a nasty slider that instantly replaced the curveball in my repertoire. After a while he told me to go run "ten poles"—five times back and forth between the left field and right field foul poles.

I weighed 240 pounds. The temperature was 105 degrees. The air felt as thick as paint. And somewhere between the fourth and seventh poles, guilt began running alongside me. I couldn't shake it. *What have I done to myself and my family? There's no way I can do this.*

In the locker room Tom Foley asked me into his office. I figured he wanted to hand me an airline ticket and say thanks but no thanks, but he handed me a pen to sign the contract and said, "Welcome to the Tampa Bay Devil Rays, Jim. Now get in shape."

This had been an audition.

Tom drove me to my motel and pointed out the areas I should avoid. It sounded like most of St. Petersburg was off-limits. He scared me. I ate dinner at Denny's across the street and jogged back to my room and called Lorri.

"I'm sorry," I said. "I'm dying. I don't think I want to do this."

She said, "I heard from Joel and some of the kids. They heard about what happened. What would you say to them if they had a door like this open for them and they didn't walk through it?" Pause. "Now, you made this decision, Jimmy. Better see what you can do with it."

For three weeks I ran every day and threw every other day. There was always a radar gun on me. The director of minor-league pitching, Chuck Hernandez, watched a few times. So did Chuck LaMar, the Rays' general manager. So did Dan Jennings. That had to mean something good, but I wouldn't let myself think so. I asked Ron Porterfield, the man in charge of training me, whether I was making a mistake. We were the same age. He said, "Hell, no. You're throwing ninety-five miles an hour. If I could do that, I'd be out there, too." I was losing eight pounds a week.

The nights were hard. Someone dropped me off at my motel and I walked to the Denny's for dinner then came back inside and locked the door and called Lorri and tried talking to the kids. Hunter was as infuriating on the phone as I am. "How ya doing?" I'd ask.

"Fine."

"Who'd you play with today?"

"Nobody."

"What did you do?"

"Nothing."

"You want to talk to me?"

"Maybe."

Jessica was more forthcoming. "I love you, Daddy," she'd say.

The Tampa Bay Devil Rays play their home games at Tropicana Field, an indoor park in St. Petersburg that looks like a giant inflated white pillow. Players often lose sight of pop-ups and fly balls against the ceiling. One night I went to a game and watched from the right field corner, fighting the urge to imagine myself as the pitcher on the mound, but sometime that week I told Lorri I was beginning to believe. The next evening I returned to my room after eating at Denny's, and the phone rang. It was Chuck Hernandez. He said the high-A team from St. Petersburg had a double-header and they wanted me to wet my feet with a couple innings of work before sending me to the double-A team in Orlando. This was my moment. In twenty-four hours I'd know if the whole thing was a fairy tale or just my own fantasy. Chuck said someone would pick me up at two-thirty and drive me to the stadium, where I'd meet the team bus for a forty-mile ride. I decided I'd wake up early and wash my clothes then.

Three hours later, at midnight, Chuck called back and woke me.

"Be packed and at the airport by eight-thirty," he said. "You're going to Zebulon, North Carolina, to meet the Orlando team."

Double-A. In six years of professional baseball, I'd never played at that level.

I got out of bed and did laundry and never fell back to sleep.

The nearest airport to Zebulon is Durham, home of the Bulls, the most famous minor-league baseball team—and the new triple-A affiliate of the Tampa Bay Devil Rays (the team used to be the high-A affiliate of the Braves' organization). I stepped off the plane, and when no one greeted me or held up a sign with my name on it, I walked to baggage claim.

My old suitcase had been replaced by a big nylon Devil Rays bag. I grabbed it off the carousel and heard a young man's voice say, "Hey, that's my bag." He was about twenty-four.

I said, "No, it's mine. Look, there's my name tag."

He said, "You're with the Devil Rays?"

I said yes, and he said, "Oh, I'm sorry, Coach."

This was worse than I'd thought. I said, "No, I'm here to pitch."

He said, "You are?"—but politely—and explained he was a pitcher, too, and had just flown back from the double-A all-star game. His bag came down the chute and we took a shuttle to the hotel.

I walked into the lobby. Tom Tisdale, the trainer, approached me. I asked if he'd been on the lookout for the old man carrying a Devil Rays bag. He said no, Ron Porterfield had told him to watch for Mike Ditka. Apparently, I'm a dead ringer. (I don't see it.)

Tom introduced me to the Orlando Rays' manager, Bill Russell. A shortstop in the 1970s and 1980s, Bill has played more games in a Los Angeles Dodgers uniform than any player, and he'd also managed the Dodgers before Fox bought the team from the O'Malley family. Bill's a no-nonsense guy, and I liked him right away because he didn't crack any old-man jokes. No doubt he'd heard tales of the fireballing grandfather but all he said was "Good to meet you. We'll be leaving for the park in about an hour and a half. Tom'll get you a uniform. See you on the bus."

Zebulon is forty miles southeast of Durham. It's home to the Carolina Mudcats. I didn't know what a Mudcat was but figured it had something to do with heat and humidity. Our clubhouse at the park was a mobile home, as hot inside as those punishment sheds you see in prison-farm movies like *Cool Hand Luke*. I walked onto the field too distracted by my own voices to have any decent memories of the field or the fans or the scoreboard or the smells. I can't even tell you what happened in the first innings. Then I collected my thoughts and decided that Bill would never put me in this game, not after my last twenty-four hours. But then he called my number. I warmed up and was sent in with one out in the seventh and a runner on first. I trotted to the mound, Bill handed me the ball and said, "All right, there it is. Let's do it," and I immediately balked by not bringing my hands to a stop in my delivery. The runner advanced to second, and I didn't dare look in the dugout.

Two pitches later the batter grounded to second, so there were now two outs but the runner was on third. I struck out the next batter and sprinted off the field and sat down on the dugout bench, sweating; I was losing water faster than a hose. No one spoke to me. That meant I'd be pitching the eighth inning, too. I faced three more batters—strikeout, pop-up, ground-out. I thought, *I can't believe it. I got in a game and actually did okay.*

Now when I ran into the dugout, several guys high-fived me. Ray Searage, the pitching coach, patted me on the back. I'd gone from a curiosity to a collector's item. In the showers I heard all the "old man" and "Grecian Formula" jokes. That meant they'd accepted me. But when the bus left us off at the hotel I showed my age by saying I wanted to hit my room and not the town. I called Lorri before falling into a coma. She said, "I knew you'd do well."

Two nights later I came in to throw the last innings

and earned the save. My fastballs averaged ninety-six. A teammate called me "The Unnatural." There was no explanation for how a man my age who'd been out of baseball for ten years and had, anyway, never thrown faster than ninety, could make skilled batters look foolish. I convinced even myself that I was for real, and when I gave up a double and a single to lose in the bottom of the ninth the following night, I surprised myself by not wanting to slit my wrists. I figured no one was perfect.

We boarded the bus and drove into the night. Our destination—Knoxville, Tennessee—was eight hours away. There were video monitors playing movies and a good air-conditioning system and a clean toilet that didn't smell. Of everyone around me, only Bill Russell could appreciate the difference between this bus and the old ones, but he'd been in the majors over twenty years, so this was slumming for him. He wanted to get back again.

I slept a few hours at the Knoxville hotel and was dressing for the bus ride to the game when Bill came in and put his hand on my shoulder. I remember exactly what I thought: *Shit!*

He said, "I've got some news for you. You leave in the morning. You have to meet Durham on the road, in Columbus."

They were sending me to triple-A. The Durham Bulls. I thought, *I'm getting a raise.*

Lorri and I desperately needed the six hundred dollars more a month that triple-A players earn, and at the moment that ranked higher than my being a few fastballs from the big leagues. I thanked Bill for everything and went off to pack.

Ted Bennett, a young lefty pitcher, heard the news and told me I might want to start thinking about hiring an agent. I laughed. What would I do with an agent? And why would he want me? He insisted, "Just talk to my agent."

He put me on with Steve Canter, in Los Angeles. I asked questions and he answered them. I liked him. He didn't stroke me. He said that if I threw as well as Ted had described, I'd be playing in Tampa Bay before the end of the season.

"The best thing you can do," he said, "is to prepare yourself for being a major-league athlete."

In the morning I flew to Columbus, home of the Yankees' triple-A affiliate, and that afternoon met another bunch of players. They seemed a little older than the double-A players, but there wouldn't be much to talk about and I wouldn't hear the Grecian Formula jokes until I showed my fastball in a game. Bill Evers, the manager, didn't put me in until the third one. He waited for me at the mound, dropped the ball in my hand, and walked away.

I threw an outside slider that didn't break enough. The batter hit a fly to the opposite field. It looked routine to me, but the wind was blowing out and I hadn't given up a home run in ten years, so my judgment was a little off. The ball landed ten rows deep in the stands.

This was a good test, and I passed it. Either maturity or God's grace allowed me to immediately forget the homer and retire the next six batters in two innings by throwing ninety-eight-mile-an-hour fastballs and a vicious slider.

I was now a bona fide Durham Bull. And this was really happening.

The bus rides weren't longer than a few hours, and home became a residence apartment twenty minutes from the ballpark in Durham. Durham was a magical place to be a minor-league baseball player. It breathes baseball. The people know the game and take credit for having America's only famous minor-league team. Signs everywhere point toward the stadium.

I stayed home most of the time, talking to Lorri on the phone and reading the Book of Proverbs, but Durham was worth exploring. You walk past old brownstones and spreading trees that remind you of Seattle until you remember that you're wet with sweat, not rain. Summer there feels like the glowing tip of a cigarette. But that's fitting. Tobacco built the town, and my sense was that it still runs things. When they erected the new stadium a few years ago across the street from an old tobacco factory, there was no doubt that the bull from the left field wall of the old stadium would be brought over and placed atop the new left field wall, or that he'd still "smoke" his giant cigarette every time a good guy hits a homer.

My pitching appearances blur together in memory. After that first one I threw well several games in a row. Then the batters began putting the bat on the ball, and Bill Evers held me out for almost two weeks. I prepared myself every afternoon but couldn't replace the negative with positive, so the time off and the question marks began eating at me.

What were their plans?

To send me back to double-A?

What if they did?

I'd say thanks anyway and go home.

At least, I hoped I would. I was thirty-five and had deserted my family to play major-league baseball, not to begin climbing a tall ladder again. Either this was meant to be, or I went home. Going home is what a mature man would have done. But maybe a few weeks' work at double-A would show me a way to complete the puzzle I'd begun thirty years ago. Maybe I'd go straight from there to the big leagues. Or would it be straight to nowhere? This was a brutal dilemma. If I stayed and sweated and still never made it, I'd always regret what it cost my family. But staying and sweating and eventually standing on a major-league mound had something to do with becoming a man. And a lot of people were rooting for that.

I called Lorri every night and we agonized together. She was in her own hell. My salary didn't cover my living expenses now, and Lorri's check couldn't cover our debts, let alone our five-hundred-dollar phone bills. Creditors pestered her mercilessly. She felt like a single parent with three kids and a crushing debt. But she told me to stay and finish the job.

So did Steve. He said, "I'd tell you to go home to your family if I thought you wouldn't get there."

"This year?" I asked.

I knew that on September first major-league teams expand their rosters from twenty-five to forty by selecting minor leaguers. The idea is to borrow some fresh help for the final month of the season, when everyone's exhausted. Teams in a pennant race choose their fifteen differently than teams like the Devil Rays. Winning teams need specific help; losing teams survey their talent. A lot of players deserve the chance to go. But only a few of them are pitchers. On our team I thought Bobby Muñoz and Terrell Wade were deserving. Muñoz stood six eight, could throw in the high nineties, and had a twelve-six curveball (think of a clock). Wade had pitched for the Braves in the World Series a few years before and now was working his way back from arm surgery. Then there was Jeff Sparks, a tall young pitcher whose style is to stumble off the mound as he throws a ruthless screwball. I would've chosen all of them over me. But none of them had my marketing value. The Devil Rays, Steve explained, were fast losing fans who'd lost interest in the losing team, and they needed a good story to tell. For the time being, that story was Wade Boggs's pursuit of three thousand hits.

"This year," Steve said. It sounded like a promise.

I don't know that I believed him until mid-August. Vince Naimoli, the managing partner of the Devil Rays, came to watch us play against Charlotte one night in Durham and asked me to sit with him in the stands behind home plate during batting practice. He's a former engineer turned businessman who in the 1980s cured several sick companies.

Chuck LaMar introduced me and sat on the other side. "Welcome to the organization," Mr. Naimoli said. "If you keep pitching the way you have been, you have a future with us."

We talked for another ten minutes, and then I ran into the outfield with the other pitchers. None of them had ever talked alone with the owner. Bobby Muñoz joked that I was a spy for management and pretended to pat me down for bugs. Terrell Wade said, "It's about time you met someone your own age."

I pitched that night. It didn't seem like a coincidence.

The first batter was Dave Hollins, a switch-hitter trying to get back to the majors after a long career there. He popped an 0-2 outside slider into the right field stands. I got the next three batters on ninety-eight-mile-an-hour fastballs, and in the dugout Bobby said, "Hollins doesn't have any power right-handed. Next time throw him inside."

I appreciated the tip. Minor-league pitchers may be friends and teammates but they're also rivals. My success would reduce Bobby's chances, and at thirty-three years old he was running out of them. So was Terrell. But we rooted for each other. We were the old family men of the team. Terrell had a wife and daughter, and Bobby had a steady girlfriend and children from a previous marriage. Every time Ricky Martin's "La Vida Loca" came on somewhere—and in the summer of 1999 it came on everywhere—Bobby would point at me and say, "That's you. Crazy life."

I pitched regularly now, and reporters wanted to talk to me. A horde of them might descend on the outfield during stretching exercises. "Here come your friends," Terrell would say. It seemed there was a story or video footage on the news every day. My favorite was Channel One, the schoolroom closed-circuit service. *Sports Illustrated* ran a short piece, and even the umpires said, "Hey, Jim, good luck. Hope this works out for you." Some nights a publicist asked me to sit in a chair after the game and sign autographs for a long line of people. Me? Jimmy Morris? Men twice my age shook my hand and said I'd inspired them. I didn't feel like anyone's inspiration. I felt like a middle-aged man who couldn't pay his bills and missed his family. That didn't seem noble or inspirational.

September first came and went with only Jeff Sparks getting called to the big club. The rest came from double-A. I'd heard that might happen. Guys said management would keep our team intact as long as we were still in a pennant race. But our season had two more weeks, leaving only two weeks on the major-league schedule. I considered those lost days to be lost opportunities and doubted that anyone felt the same pressure, because no one else intended to walk away if the call didn't come. There were nights I sat on my knees in prayer. I didn't pray for success or a 0.00 ERA, or a bundle of money. I prayed to be shown my right path.

"God, if this isn't what I'm supposed to be doing, then please show me what it is I'm supposed to be doing. Give me a sign."

There were two possible signs. One was the call-up. The other was an arm injury. No third possibility occurred to me, and I braced for failure. Bobby asked me to drive back to Texas with him.

The season ended with three games against Charlotte, our competition for the International League championship and the only team that had had my number. We won the first two games and needed to win the third but were behind three to one when I came in to pitch the seventh and blew away all three batters.

Bobby pitched the eighth. He did well and joined me afterward in the locker room to see what developed. We were mapping our route to Texas when the game ended with Charlotte as champs.

Then time seemed to stop. The next thirty minutes would write the story of my life. Did I want to know the outcome? Or would it be better to fantasize, like the way you check a Lotto ticket against the numbers?

I sat alone in front of my locker, half in the present and half in outer space, and in my periphery noticed Bill Evers. He walked behind me—damn!—then tapped me on the shoulder, and as he kept walking whispered, "I've got some other people to talk to first, but after I talk to them, I want you to come in my office." He saw the look on my face and added, "It's not bad news."

I nodded and showered and dressed and waited by my locker again. "Not bad news" was different from "good news." "Not bad news" could mean they weren't cutting me but wanted me to come back and try this next year. A steady stream of "not good news" faces filed out of Bill's office.

Steve Cox and I were called in at the same time. This could only mean good news. Steve was the most valuable player in the International League that season. Scott Proefrock, an assistant general manager, sat next to Bill.

"It's all right, Jimmy," Scott said, "you can smile now."

Bill said, "You're going to the big leagues."

The time was 10:30 P.M., on Friday, September 17, 1999. The moment that was never going to come was now here, but it didn't seem entirely real and wouldn't until I shared it with my family.

Bill explained we'd be flying out early to meet the Devil Rays on the road. Of all the possible teams in the American League, the Devil Rays were scheduled against the Rangers. The Texas Rangers. In Arlington, Texas, just outside Dallas.

Everyone I loved could come.

I walked back to my locker and tried not to smile in front of young men whose hearts were broken. Bobby said, "I'm driving back by myself, aren't I?" and shook my hand. Terrell hugged me. I felt bad for both of them.

In the hotel room I called Lorri. A baby-sitter answered and said she didn't know what time Lorri would be home. I called Mom, but Charles said she was on the road, driving to meet a friend in Branson, Missouri; he told me eight times how proud he was. Then I called Dad, who said, "I told you so," and promised to be at the game the next day. I called Lorri again. Still not home. I was mad and frustrated now. How could she not be home? I left a message with the baby-sitter, relating a list of things I wanted her to bring to Arlington without saying why I was going to be there.

Lorri phoned back at midnight her time and said, "What's this about? What do you need new suitcases for?"

I said, "Because I only have those ugly old things. And I don't want the major leaguers to think I'm a hick."

"What're you saying?"

"I got called up."

"Jimmy, this isn't funny," she said. "It's too late and I'm not in the mood to joke."

I said, "No, really, I did, no joke," and told her the story of being in Evers's office.

Lorri screamed and then came back to her senses and we talked and cried and finally she said she couldn't leave early in the morning with the kids because she had to administer an admissions test, the same one she'd given three months before, on that Saturday of my tryout. It was after midnight now, too late to find a substitute proctor, but she promised they'd all be there before game time. When we hung up, she phoned Whack's house in Big Lake, waking everyone, and soon after sunup Whack drove slowly through town, honking his horn and shouting out the window, "Coach made it! Coach Morris made it!"

An hour of sleep and a three-hour flight later, I found myself in the lobby of an Arlington hotel among thirty-nine other major-league players. Wade Boggs, a future Hall of Famer, hugged me and said mine was the best story he'd ever heard. Fred McGriff hugged me, too, and Jose Canseco shook my hand. I reminded myself to record details in my brain—faces, smells, colors, the way I felt—but everything looked too new. The best you can hope for in that situation is not to stutter or stumble.

We boarded the bus and in a few minutes approached Arlington Stadium. The players call it one of the prettiest in the country, a retro park designed after baseball's glory days, but with more creature comforts. The bus disappeared into a tunnel and let us off in the stadium's belly. It was a short walk to the locker room.

My eyes fell on a locker that read "Jim Morris" in black, bold pen, and inside the locker hung a uniform, a Tampa Bay Devil Rays uniform, number 63, a major-league uniform for me to wear in a major-league game—and my name was written across the back. I'd never dressed more slowly or taken more pleasure in it. I didn't notice whose lockers were next to mine.

Larry Rothschild, the manager, greeted me. He'd been the pitching coach for the Florida Marlins when they won the World Series. He didn't say anything about pitching that night, and I figured he'd let me adjust to reality for a day or two before throwing me in the water. Besides, I'd pitched the night before and the night before that. I hoped Lorri and the kids wouldn't be too disappointed seeing me not get in the game. I hoped the will-call window had their tickets. I hoped they'd found the stadium. I hoped they hadn't been killed in an accident.

We stretched on the field and warmed up, and the pitchers shagged flies in batting practice. I couldn't stop gaping. I was on a major-league field. And the stands were filling up with 37,000 people to root for their team in a pennant race. Thirty-seven thousand. I'd never seen that many people in one place. Finding Lorri would be impossible.

Game time was in ten minutes. The other pitchers and I took seats in the right field bullpen. I thought I heard my name called, but wasn't sure until someone elbowed me and pointed up at Lorri. I recognized her with my heart, not my eyes. She'd been turned back by ushers who mistook her for a groupie, and had to sneak through them.

Lorri had never seen me in uniform and we hadn't been together for three months. "Oh, Jimmy," she said. Tears rolled down her cheeks, and then rolled down my cheeks. I stood up and stepped over and grabbed her. It was an epic, swaying hug. People applauded. Lorri pointed toward their seats and promised to be waiting outside the locker room after the game, and "The Star-Spangled Banner" put a baseball-sized lump in my throat.

I didn't watch much of the game. There wasn't much of a game to watch. Our starting pitching allowed several runs early, deflating any tension in the bullpen, of which there wasn't much anyway, with the team half a season back in the standings and playing now only to spoil the Rangers' pennant push. Good thing, too. Because for the first time in nearly thirty-six years I needed and wanted to talk—to talk with my new teammates and to think of them as human so that I could think of myself as one of them. We talked about hometowns and hobbies and girlfriends and wives, and they all asked to hear my story and shook their heads when they heard it. Guys described the Devil Rays' terrible season of injuries and disappointments, and someone predicted big roster changes for next year. Next year? What about this year?

In the sixth inning the bullpen phone rang. Larry Rothschild wanted Jeff Sparks to get loose. I slapped Jeff on the rear and wished him luck as he ran out to pitch, and he pitched well in the seventh. In the top of the eighth the call came for Mike Duvall to warm up, and forty seconds later the phone rang again. For me.

"Me?" I asked. "You sure?"

They laughed.

I grabbed my mitt. The temperature was 103 degrees. It took four pitches to loosen up. But I kept throwing. Pitching was the only thing that felt normal now.

In the inning Jeff got two outs before allowing a

eighth single to Tom Goodwin. Larry walked out to the mound and touched his left arm.

He wanted Jim Morris.

The bullpen gate swung open. I began jogging in. It was the jog I'd made ten thousand times in my mind, but different. The stadium seemed too big and the crowd sounded like cannon fire and my heart beat hard and fast enough to flutter my jersey.

On the mound, Larry dropped the ball in my mitt. We were behind six to one, so this wasn't about winning or losing. He wanted to see what I'd brought.

"Can you throw strikes?" he said.

I said, "I'll try." He laughed and walked to the dugout.

John Flaherty, the catcher, asked, "What do you throw?"

"Fastball and slider," I said.

"One and three," he said, trotting back to the plate. He'd signal one for fastball, three for slider.

All I had to do was get one out and walk off the mound. I thought, *I hope I don't balk. I hope I don't throw the ball to the backstop. I hope I don't fall down.*

The batter was Royce Clayton, the Rangers' shortstop; he already had two hits in the game. John squatted down behind home and I stared in for the signal. He showed one finger. Fastball.

I went into my stretch and glanced over at Tom Goodwin, taking a lead off first base. He'd stolen his thirty-seventh base in the second inning, and there was a good chance he'd try to steal on the nervous newbie, but there wasn't a chance in the world that I'd throw over there to pick him off. The ball would have sailed into the dugout. No, what happened now was strictly between me and Royce Clayton, a twenty-nine-year-old veteran of eight major-league seasons and a thirty-five-year-old rookie.

First pitch was a strike, low and away, ninety-six miles an hour.

John liked what he saw and again put down a single finger.

Second pitch was a strike, low and away, ninety-eight miles an hour.

John put down a single finger.

Third pitch was a strike, low and away, ninety-eight miles an hour. Royce caught a small piece and fouled it weakly along the first base line. The count was still 0-2.

John put down a single finger, then pointed upward. He wanted a high fastball.

I gave it to him. Ninety-eight miles an hour. It came in at Royce's chest. He checked his swing and John appealed to the first-base umpire. Yes, his bat had crossed the plate.

Strike three!

There was a brief delay between what my eyes saw and what my brain registered, like watching a golfer strike the ball and hearing the *thwack* a second later.

And I was encased in silence, hearing only white noise.

John jogged toward our dugout and I followed. Jeff Sparks was standing on the top step. He hugged me and shouted, "You did it, dude. You did it."

I stepped down and slapped high-fives and a dozen guys put their arms around me.

"Hey, old guy," a voice said.

I turned around. It was John, still in his catcher's gear.

"You might want this," he said, tossing me the strikeout ball. "Welcome to the major leagues."

EPILOGUE

MAYBE THE REASON I never liked fairy tales was that I wondered what followed "And they lived happily ever after. . . ." What followed for me was miraculous.

Lorri and the kids met me in the locker room. My wife and I held each other to within an inch of injury. We talked about finding someplace fancy to celebrate, but the kids were hungry for pizza, so we met at the hotel and they fell asleep before Pizza Hut arrived. That meant Lorri and I could find each other. In its way it was the perfect celebration. At one point I was in the bathroom and could hear her laughing. On television, the Rangers' manager, Johnny Oates, was devoting all of his postgame comments to me. Then sportscasters on ESPN and other stations dug into history books and found that I was the oldest rookie since thirty-six-year-old Minnie Mendoza first played for the Minnesota Twins in 1970; the difference was that he'd never been out of baseball.

Two days later Lorri was at the bus before we left for the airport and our flight to Anaheim. Larry Rothschild asked her, "Do you mind if we borrow him for a while?"

"You've had him longer than I have," she said before kissing me goodbye.

Our next three games were against the Angels. On the morning of the first game the *Los Angeles Times* ran a long piece about me, written by its top sports columnist, Bill Plaschke. The moment that edition hit the streets, Steve Canter's phone started ringing and didn't stop for months. Television and radio and newspapers wanted interviews, and studios and publishing houses wanted to buy my story. The movie rights went to the Walt Disney Co., and Little, Brown contracted me to write this book.

When the season ended, the Devil Rays sent me to the Arizona fall league, the one for top prospects only. In six weeks I had an ERA of zero and a fastball that timed hotter than one hundred miles an hour.

I left Arizona more worn down than tired, anxious to see my family. Checks would be coming now, enough to pay off our debts and then some, but there were no guarantees about the future, so Lorri couldn't quit her job. Not that she would have, anyway. She earns more satisfaction from it than money.

My fifteen minutes of fame were demanding. Reporters and camera crews called with persistence, and suddenly I had some "business interests," as Steve said. I gave speeches to civic groups and schools and churches and synagogues. I traveled to Los Angeles and New York and Florida. And all the while I wondered where I'd be next year and what I'd be doing.

Would I make the major-league roster? Would I quit baseball if they sent me back to the minors? There'd be no answers until spring training ended in early April. That gave us almost five months of uncertainty. It didn't sit well.

I was home too few days, and of those, too few were just days meant for family. In early February I drove from San Angelo to St. Petersburg and reported weeks early to spring training.

For two months I lived in a small residence motel and worked my thirty-six-year-old body and arm into shape. The competition for the role of "situational lefty" in the bullpen was strong, and when I boarded the team plane for Minneapolis, where the season was to begin, I believed that management had other plans for me. But somewhere over northern Florida, Larry

Rothschild walked past me in the aisle and casually said, "You're on the twenty-five," meaning the twenty-five-man roster. I was a major-league ballplayer.

Imagine a club, a members-only club. It's one of the most exclusive in the world. You've wanted to belong all your life. And now, suddenly, you do—not just for two weeks but for a whole season, and maybe the season after that and the ones to follow. Sure, I could be sent down at any time, or even cut, but some people said I threw one of the best sliders in the majors.

I didn't handle things as gracefully as I might have. I'd vowed to remember who I was, in the way my grandfather meant, but I sometimes forgot to be James Morris Jr., instead of a major-league baseball player. And without Lorri and the kids as an anchor, I drifted a little and fell into old, bad habits.

Lorri and I could not connect. Our worlds seemed separated by worlds. I pitched in Camden Yards and Fenway Park and Yankee Stadium, places where they wrote baseball history. What felt real were the fields and my teammates. My wife's voice over the phone sounded far, far away.

By April Lorri and I had been apart almost nine of the last ten months. She and the kids flew out for Easter weekend, but we were like two positive magnetic poles forced apart by invisible energy. We vowed to try again, on Mother's Day weekend.

On the Wednesday night before that Sunday, the

Devil Rays played the Yankees, in New York. Larry called me in to pitch to Paul O'Neill with two outs and the bases loaded in the bottom of the tenth.

I jogged to the mound feeling less than perfect and fearing something was wrong. A stiff back and a tired, sore elbow had been dogging me since our new pitching coach decided to have me throw in the bullpen on game days, believing that it would improve my control. In the last five days I'd been up and throwing nine times. And now I couldn't get loose.

Paul O'Neill bats left-handed. This was exactly the situation, facing a lefty in a key moment, for which the Devil Rays employed me. Most of the time I'd come through; lefties were hitting only .167 against me. But that night I threw four straight pitches outside of the strike zone to walk in the winning run. Instead of ninety-five-mile-an-hour rockets, I was throwing eighty-five-mile lobs.

Two days later the organization sent me to Durham. My arm still ached when I came in to pitch a horrible inning on the night after Mother's Day. That one inning ended my season and possibly my career. My elbow needed surgery.

You might call that depressing. I don't. I think it was God's hand steering me again to the right place.

The right place was home.

The injury had led to my poor performance, leading to my demotion, leading to the surgeon's table and a flight home to my wife four months earlier than if I'd played the whole season. You can't get luckier than that. Another four months apart would have left us with nothing to repair and no desire to try.

I sometimes imagine myself at death's door, sorting through memories like souvenirs. I know I'll remember people and places and dogs. I'll remember the long road to my dream and all the turns and obstacles along the way. I'll remember standing on a major-league mound and striking out Royce Clayton and Mo Vaughn and Frank Thomas, and I'll smile because I won't have to regret losing my wife and family to a dream that I learned didn't mean as much to me as they did.